Ian Carmichael speaks into our
ness, and charts the only road to
more tips on time managemer
about who we are as humans,
busyness in his plan of redemptic
slaves to busyness because we do

disarmingly honest, confronting and warmly conversational
at the same time, anticipating our questions and objections.
He provides very practical reflections for personal change
towards godly busyness for employees, church members,
parents, children, husbands, wives and siblings. I can see
radical implications for how we think about retirement.
This book is comprehensive.

Colin Marshall
Author, *Growth Groups* and *Passing the Baton*
Co-author, *The Trellis and the Vine* and *The Vine Project*

Ian Carmichael's book *Busy* is refreshingly clear and to the
point. It helps us re-examine the purpose of life while we
wait for the new creation—that is, Christ-directed busyness
and rest. Ian's relationship audit exercise is insightful and
practical for applying the biblical principles given in the first
half of the book:

Step 1:   Identify our key relationships.

Step 2:   Reflect on how we can be more intentional in
          seeing these precious people transferred into
          God's kingdom and transformed into the like-
          ness of Jesus.

Medical experts recommend booking annual health checks.
I recommend buying and reading this book as an excellent
yearly spiritual health check.

Carmelina Read
Dean of Women, Christ College, Sydney

Ian Carmichael's *Busy* is a wonderful read. It's full of biblical wisdom, warmth, humour and grace. Most importantly it will help you think about how God's kindness in Jesus rearranges our priorities and helps us be busy in a healthy way for God. It's a book born of a life lived serving Jesus and putting the Bible into practice. It's a book that will encourage you to rest in God, work hard for Christ, and put busyness into perspective. I encourage you to grab a copy, read it, and live it! It might just turn 'busy' into joyful service.

Paul Grimmond
Dean of Students and Lecturer in Ministry and
Mission, Moore Theological College, Sydney

Busy is not what I expected but it's exactly what I needed, and I suspect it's what many of us need. Challenging me to rethink not only Monday-Fridays, Ian also really pushed me to think again about my Sundays (and I say this as a pastor!). I pray this book will be given to every Christian, from new to mature, with the hope that all of them will consider how they themselves are answers to the prayer of Matthew 9:37-38 —a call to be busy with work for the harvest.

Marty Sweeney
Pastor of Training, Old North Church, Ohio
Executive Director, Matthias Media, USA

Busy

TACKLING THE PROBLEM OF AN
OVERLOADED CHRISTIAN LIFE

Ian Carmichael

SYDNEY · YOUNGSTOWN

Matthias Media
(St Matthias Press Ltd ACN 067 558 365)
Email: info@matthiasmedia.com.au
Internet: www.matthiasmedia.com.au
Please visit our website for current postal and telephone contact information.

Matthias Media (USA)
Email: sales@matthiasmedia.com
Internet: www.matthiasmedia.com
Please visit our website for current postal and telephone contact information.

ISBN 978 1 925424 84 3

Cover design by Georgia Condie.
Typesetting by Lankshear Design.

~ For Steph, Lauren and Glen ~
with the prayer that they will continue to rest in,
but be busy with, God's work.

Contents

Introduction

I wonder why you picked up this book.

I'm reasonably sure it's not because you saw my name on the front cover. Given this is my first book, I'm unlikely to feature on your list of favourite authors.[1]

More likely the word 'busy' caught your eye.

Is that because you're not particularly busy, and you're a little worried that you may have meandered into laziness?

I guess that's *possible*. And if that's why you picked up this book, you'll be glad to know it will help you. It's not a book just for busy people.

But my hunch is that this is actually going to be an uncommon reason for picking up the book.

More likely, you picked it up because you feel like the word in big letters on the cover is a somewhat overused one in your vocabulary. When people ask, "How are you?", the word 'busy' is one you regularly offer in response. Perhaps you say, "Really busy" or "Crazy busy". Or even "Flat out like a lizard drinking!", to quote one of my favourite

---

1   But feel free to reassess this at the end of the book!

Aussie colloquialisms.

If so, do you see 'busy' as a good thing to be? Or when you say it, is there a sense of "I actually wish my life wasn't this busy"? Perhaps there's a slight discontent brewing within you about the way your life is panning out? Or even a desire for change but with no obvious way to achieve it?

And if you do have a sense that your life is too busy, how do you think about it *as a Christian*?

Is being a follower of Jesus, and your involvement in church life, part of the problem or part of the solution?

Does being a Christian add an extra layer of activity and responsibility to an already full life?[2]

Do you ever secretly daydream about what your life would be like if you *weren't* a Christian, and how much less busy you might feel? You'd certainly have more time to relax on a Sunday. Maybe on weekdays you could also sleep in an extra 20 minutes instead of getting up early to read the Bible and pray. Or you could relax and watch more Netflix in the evenings instead of diligently teaching the Bible to your kids and then preparing for your Bible study group on Wednesday night.

Again, my hunch is that living as a Christian, for most of us, feels like it adds to the problem.

Or maybe you picked up this book not because of the *quantity* of your busyness, but the *quality*. Perhaps many of your routine activities feel somewhat like trivial pursuits, and it's hard to find any deep satisfaction or fulfilment in

---

2   I'm pretty sure that's not what Jesus had in mind when he said "I have come that they may have life, and have it to the full" (John 10:10, NIV).

them. Maybe you want to attach a generator to the hamster wheel of your life so that all that running around gives a greater sense of actually achieving something.

Or maybe you're on the edge of burnout, or recovering from it and wanting to make sure you don't end up there again. Or maybe there is someone in your life you are worried about and want to help.

Whatever your reasons, why not pause here for a moment and pray that God will use this book to help address the issues you're concerned about?

Not the magic bullet

Now, I've read enough self-help books and the advertising for them to know how the normal schtick ought to go for a book about busyness:

> I was too busy to write this book. Every day was spent madly trying to juggle too many balls in the air at once—and failing. *But now*, after years of research, experimentation and deep reflection, I've discovered a method to get an astounding amount done, leaving you with a 3-hour work week and plenty of leisure time. As a one-time special offer, you get the full method, plus a collection of dubious-but-inspirational anecdotes, all for the crazy, never-to-be-repeated price of just $~~499.00~~ $29.99.

In other words, the magic bullet offered is generally a quick fix methodology for you to implement. You're given tips on time management, productivity, learning how to say 'no', delegation, keeping your email inbox under control, and so on. Perhaps with a bit of reassuring pop psychology thrown in for good measure.

The better books might go a little bit deeper. They might ask you to think about what you *want* out of life. What lifestyle are you looking for? What do you want to achieve? Then they give you the techniques and strategies designed to help you achieve those life goals (no matter what they are).

But what I want to do is a bit different again.

I want to avoid magic bullets and instead look with you at what *God* has to say in the Bible about busyness.

By which I don't mean looking for a verse in the book of Proverbs that says something vaguely connected with productivity and using it as a pretext to say what I wanted to say about productivity anyway.

No, I mean going to the Bible in search of answers to some of the most fundamental questions about our life's meaning and purpose—what God created us to *do*—and seeing what implications that has for our lives.

Warning

Now I have to warn you, as we explore some of these big Bible truths, you might at times wonder how on earth it's all connected to your daily struggles with overwhelming busyness (or your lack of struggle).

Stick with me at those points.

Ultimately the riches of God's word will greatly help us, not just in explaining our experience of life, but in wisely shaping the way we live it. That well-worn Bible verse on the poster is in fact profoundly true: "Your word is a lamp to my feet and a light to my path" (Ps 119:105).

In the end, what we discover from the Bible will provide you with a much deeper and clearer picture—a better framework for making decisions. It will help you make the mind-numbing number of choices you need to make each week about what to do with your time.

I promise all these big thoughts *will* ultimately get very practical ... just not necessarily in quite the way you might be expecting![3]

For some people, busyness is a useful smokescreen: "My life must be meaningful and of high value—look how busy and in demand I am!" Being busy can cover up a deep existential hollowness.

For Christians, that shouldn't be the case. We know a purpose and a meaning that comes from our Creator and his plan for our world. It's a meaning that gives our lives direction and value.

But it's still possible for us to be so busy as to lose sight of that bigger picture. Or, for that matter, to 'not see the forest for the trees' as we engage with God's word, the Bible.

So my prayer is that as you keep turning the pages of this book, you will see—with new or renewed clarity—the biblical bigger picture of which you are a part. And that you will then be equipped to prayerfully make wise changes to your life, for your own good, for the good of others around you, and to the glory of God.

---

3   But what have you got to lose? This book costs even less than $29.99.

Some housekeeping

Three quick things to point out to you as you get started:

1. At the end of each chapter there are reflection questions for you to do to push you to personally apply what you are reading. I know it's easy to skip past the questions. But I urge you to invest the time in them to get the most benefit.

2. I don't know about you, but when I read a book, by the time I get to chapter 5, I've largely forgotten what the main points were in chapters 1, 2, 3 and even 4. So I've also included a summary statement at the end of each chapter—a summary we'll add to as we go along. Hopefully that will help you follow the logic of the book.

3. I worked for 33 years for Matthias Media, the publisher of this book, and I am still involved in their ministry in an honorary capacity. Naturally I know their books and resources extremely well. So when I suggest further reading on a topic, I almost always recommend something from Matthias Media. Please bear with me on that. I know it's even less subtle than Apple's product placement in movies, but these are the resources I know and the ones that theologically connect well with the ideas in this book. I don't get any kickback, I assure you.

1.
Made in God's image

No self-respecting evangelical book with any credibility fails to quote John Calvin at some point. So let's get it done nice and early:

> But though the knowledge of God and the knowledge of ourselves are bound together by a mutual tie, due arrangement requires that we treat of the former in the first place, and then descend to the latter.[4]

In other words, to understand ourselves, Calvin suggests we start with an understanding of our Creator—his character and his purposes. For reasons we will see, God provides the right foundation for developing an accurate self-understanding.

That's what we're going to do in this chapter and the next two: start with God and see where that leads us in understanding ourselves.

---

4   J Calvin, *Institutes of the Christian Religion* (H Beveridge trans), book 1, chapter 1, Bonham Norton, 1599 (reformed.org/books/institutes/books/book1/bk1ch01.html).

And we can start at the very beginning, because as soon as we open our Bibles, right there on the opening pages, a profound truth is drilled into us over and over again: God is the Creator (Gen 1:1; cf. Rev 4:11; Ps 33:6-9; and many other places).

Straight away that tells us something very significant about ourselves: we are his creatures. He made us. We are made.

Difference

That means God is in a very different category to us. In this world there is a category of 'all-powerful God'—and you and me, we're not in that category.

That sounds obvious, I know. But it's worth saying because—from Genesis 3 and the rest of the Bible, and also from personal experience—we know we have a hard time accepting that we're *not* God. We keep rejecting him as the God who rightly rules his creation and ought to be obeyed. We keep pretending *we* are in charge. When you think about it, that's pretty silly—not to mention offensive to God. But we'll talk more about solving that problem in a future chapter.

The point for the moment is that there is a fundamental difference between us and God. As the apostle Paul puts it, it's the stark difference between the potter and the clay (Rom 9:21). God is God; we are very much *not* God. He is the infinite, all-powerful, all-wise, all-knowing Creator of everything. We, on the other hand, are very finite creatures he has made for his own purposes. It is the potter who defines the nature and purpose of his clay creation. The clay awaits the potter's hands and takes on the role the potter gives to it.

Similarity

But although there is a *very significant difference*, at the same time—and exclusively out of all of God's creation—there is also a very significant *similarity* between us and God. This particular creature—the human—is uniquely made in God's image, in his likeness:

> Then God said, "Let us make man in our image, after our likeness. And let them have dominion over the fish of the sea and over the birds of the heavens and over the livestock and over all the earth and over every creeping thing that creeps on the earth."
>
> So God created man in his own image,
> > in the image of God he created him;
> > male and female he created them.
>
> And God blessed them. And God said to them, "Be fruitful and multiply and fill the earth and subdue it, and have dominion over the fish of the sea and over the birds of the heavens and over every living thing that moves on the earth." (Gen 1:26-28)

Theologians have debated for years about what it means for man to be made "in the image of God". But one meaning is pretty simple: an image of something reveals aspects of that something. The better the image, the more it reveals.

If I show you my holiday snap of the Grand Canyon, you and I both know that my 5x7-inch photo doesn't do justice to the scale and wonder of the real thing. But it's undeniably still an image giving you at least *some* idea of what the Grand Canyon is like in real life.

So it's not my photo that gives meaning to the Grand Canyon; it's the canyon that gives meaning and significance to my photo. When you look at that photo and ask me "What's that?", I will say "It's the Grand Canyon", or, if I'm being particularly pedantic, "It's a photo of the Grand Canyon". If I say "It's a piece of paper with ink on it" you'll most likely just roll your eyes at me.

In the same way, as God's image-bearers we derive our meaning and significance from him. But in doing so, we reflect real truths about God, even with our fallen nature.[5]

As God's image-bearers we are uniquely designed and created to reveal aspects of God's own nature and purpose.[6]

I don't know if you've ever thought about it like this, but in Romans the apostle Paul says that the creation offers enough evidence to allow all people to clearly per-

---

5 It is worth noting that one of the issues theologians wrestle with is to what extent we continue to be in the image of God after the Fall in Genesis 3. Generally it is agreed that something of that image is retained, because it is referred to in post-Fall contexts like Genesis 5:3 (where Seth is in the image of Adam, who is in the image of God) and 9:6, 1 Corinthians 11:7 and James 3:9. But the image is certainly marred and corrupted by sin, and needs restoration (see Rom 8:29; Eph 4:22-24; 1 Cor 15:49; 2 Cor 3:18; Col 3:10). In that sense, it is another point of difference between us and God: he is righteous, whereas our nature is to rebel and resist his will. It will become more and more obvious in this book why our reluctance to submit to God's sovereign control of the narrative is a problem for us.

6 Perhaps that's why one of the first jobs we were given was to "multiply"—a job we seem to have been unusually good at. How shrewd and generous of God to build in so much job satisfaction for that task.

ceive God's "invisible attributes" (Rom 1:20). And we, as the only creatures made in God's image and the pinnacle of his creation, are not only *part* of that testimony about God's attributes; we could be considered the most *accurate* and *revealing* part.

In other words, although there is a fundamental *difference* between us and God, God has also built into his creation—and for the fulfilment of his divine purposes—an astonishing and profoundly significant *similarity* between us and God.

Both the differences and the similarities help us discover who we are and who we are meant to be.

Indeed, very helpfully to us as we explore our topic of busyness, the differences and similarities are very much at play in the areas of our work and rest. So we're going to explore those areas in our next two chapters.

Reflection

1. When you reflect on the busyness of your life, what are some of the principles or values that you bring to the topic? Do you think there is a distinctly 'Christian' view of busyness, or as you start this book are you sceptical that the Bible really has very much to say on it?

2. We are "the only creatures made in God's image and the pinnacle of his creation". Read Psalm 8. About what does the psalmist express amazement (in terms of the relationship between us and God)? Does it amaze you?

3. Why do you think God chose to make part of his creation "in his own image" (Gen 1:27)?

Chapter by chapter summary	
1	God is our Creator and we are made in his image. We are like him, but also different.
2	
3	
4	
5	
6	
7	
8	
9	
10	
11	

2.
Made in God's image to work

A friend sent me a meme this morning which said, "You never realize how weird you are until you have a kid who acts just like you." Like many memes, this amusingly expresses a deep truth: we are often very like our parents, and if we have kids they are very often like us. Perhaps embarrassingly so—in both directions.

But it's also true that we can be very different. (I imagine my kids cling desperately to that hope!)

In analysing those familial similarities and differences, we can actually gain some very useful insights about ourselves. You should try it sometime.

But, as we have just seen in chapter 1, something similar goes on with us and God our Creator. Amazingly, we are made in his image—in some ways like him, and in other ways different. And by reflecting on his character and purpose—both the similarities and the differences—we can learn important things about *our* character and purpose.

So what else do we know about God, in addition to him being our Creator?

God the worker

One of the very next things we learn about God when we open our Bibles is that he is a *worker*.

In Genesis 1, God creates the world. And chapter 2 describes that creative act as God's "work" (v 2). You might even say that God has been busy. And to this day he continues to be busily at work in the world (Josh 24:31; John 5:17), sustaining it by his powerful word (Heb 1:3; Matt 5:45, 10:29-30; Psalm 104; Col 1:17).

Now, at this point, it's probably worth pausing briefly to notice that these days we use the word 'work' in a number of different ways. Most commonly, we use it to talk about our paid employment—for example, "I'm off to work".

Clearly what God has been doing in Genesis 1 is not 'paid employment'. Work in this context means something more general. It is more like 'purposeful activity'. Or busyness.

Whilst paid employment is, for many of us, one of the main activities that contribute to our busyness, it is certainly not the only 'work' we do. So, for example, you might be studying, or caring for children at home, or learning a musical instrument: that's all purposeful activity, just as much as paid employment.

As we discuss busyness in this book, we'll be talking about all sorts of activities and ways of spending our time. So I'm going to try to avoid using the term 'work' where I possibly can.[7] But it's a word our English translations of the Bible often use, so at some points its use in this book is unavoidable. But at least we now all know we're defining it pretty broadly.

Now, back to the main point.

Our similarity

So God is a worker. And here's the *similarity*: when God creates the man and woman in his image, he gives them work to do as well:

> The LORD God took the man and put him in the garden of Eden to work it and keep it. (Gen 2:15)[8]

So God the worker creates men and women to be like him as workers. Their particular role is to work the garden and take care of it.

As a result, we can say that having things to do reflects God's own purposefulness and is a part of God's good created order. God's plan was for us to work—to *do* stuff. And that plan continues after the Fall and outside the garden.[9]

---

7 Appendix 1, which is specifically about paid employment, is an exception.

8 The man is given the work to do before the woman is made. But she is then given the role of being a "helper" to the man (Gen 2:18). So I take it that both Adam and Eve are workers.

9 The continuing role of humans as workers is apparent as early as Genesis 4:12, when God refers to Cain's ongoing work in his pronouncement of the curse: "When you work the ground, it shall no longer yield to you its strength".

Our difference

But ... as workers there is also a fundamental *difference* between God and us.

God the Creator is all-powerful. He speaks and it happens. For example, in doing his work of creating the world, "God said, 'Let there be ...' and there was" (e.g. Gen 1:3).

God is never frustrated because he can't achieve what he wants to achieve:

> "I know that you can do all things,
>> and that no purpose of yours can be thwarted."
>>> (Job 42:2)

His word—by which he does his work—does not fail to accomplish what he intends:

> "For as the rain and the snow come down from heaven
>> and do not return there but water the earth,
> making it bring forth and sprout,
>> giving seed to the sower and bread to the eater,
> so shall my word be that goes out from my mouth;
>> it shall not return to me empty,
> but it shall accomplish that which I purpose,
>> and shall succeed in the thing for which I sent it." (Isa 55:10-11)

But that's not true of you or me, is it?

In fact, in the book of Ecclesiastes the Teacher reminds us of what it's like to be a creature in this fallen world of painful toil under the curse that God has imposed (Gen 3:17-19):

> So I hated life, because what is done under the sun
> was grievous to me, for all is vanity and a striving
> after wind. (Eccl 2:17)

There is a frustration to the life of a creature—we're not in control. We can be extremely busy, diligently pursuing our cherished goals, and in the end it can prove to be a total chasing after the wind, all in vain, and nothing short of pointless. If you've not yet experienced that in your paid employment, well ... I hope you are enjoying your first day in your first job.

But our frustration is not solely caused by our relative powerlessness. We are also *sinful*. Our human nature is to reject God's control. So we are battling against God for control, and that's not a battle we will win.[10] It's a little like the feeling you get in a sporting contest against someone who is a much better player than you. Try as you might, you just can't achieve what you're hoping for, and it can be extremely frustrating.

Yet the Bible is not entirely negative about the fact that our toil is subject to frustration. We can still find a God-given satisfaction in our activities and busyness. The same Teacher says:

> There is nothing better for a person than that he
> should eat and drink and find enjoyment in his toil.
> This also, I saw, is from the hand of God, for apart
> from him who can eat or who can have enjoyment?
> (Eccl 2:24-25)

10 Fortunately! I shudder to think what the world would be like if my will prevailed over God's.

In fact, the Bible sees busyness and industriousness as very positive virtues and is decidedly negative about idleness and laziness (Prov 6:6, 13:4, 31:10-31; 1 Tim 5:13; Matt 25:14-30; 2 Thess 3:6-13). Frustration is not seen as a reason for giving up work.

Indeed, a lack of busyness can open up the temptation to sin, with the sin of becoming "gossips and busybodies" particularly singled out (1 Tim 5:13; cf. 2 Thess 3:11). If you want to learn more about the potential dangers of *not* being busy, you can also head to the book of Proverbs and search for what it says there about the "sluggard".[11]

Activity and busyness are seen as positive partly because they are a means of blessing others. For example, the apostle Paul says each of us should be "doing honest work with his own hands, so that he may have something to share with anyone in need" (Eph 4:28). In the Bible busyness is only seen as a negative thing if it is misdirected—if it pursues evil ends or results in us neglecting the good responsibilities and relationships that God himself gives us.

So the bottom line is this: **well-directed busyness is actually a good thing**. It reflects the nature of God as a worker, and the truth that "whatever you do" can be done "as for the Lord" (Col 3:23).

In other words, busyness is not necessarily the enemy. Busyness is definitely not a dirty word.

But there is more to say—some of which we will dis-

---

11 The ESV and NIV use the word 'sluggard'. But I do enjoy the more modern way the Christian Standard Bible translates it as 'slacker'.

cover in the next chapter, as we think about the fact that God the worker also *rests*.

Reflection

1. The apostle Paul says we should warn those who are idle (1 Thess 5:14). So are you busy enough? Do you have an idleness problem?[12] What can you do about it?

2. In what ways do you find your busyness or work to be hard and frustrating? What causes that frustration?

3. In what ways do you find your busyness or work satisfying? What causes that satisfaction?

4. How well do you "share with anyone in need" (Eph 4:28) the blessings that come from your own work/busyness?

12 Proverbs 6:10 warns against idleness and the dangers of "a little sleep, a little slumber, a little folding of the hands to rest ..." To which maybe we should add the modern downtime pursuits: "... a little Facebook, a little Netflix, a little gaming". What do you think?

Chapter by chapter summary	
1	God is our Creator and we are made in his image. We are like him, but also different.
2	God works; he is busy. God gives us, his image-bearers, work to do. Work or busyness is a good thing if it is well-directed.
3	
4	
5	
6	
7	
8	
9	
10	
11	

3.
Made in God's image to rest

How was your day? Did it feel long? If so, take a moment to sympathize with any lifeforms on Venus. One day for them lasts for 243 of our Earth days, and that's a lot of time for activity.[13] On the other hand, it puts a whole new spin on having a long weekend.

I don't think I'm cut out for life on Venus. But, happily, 24 hours in a day seems about right. It's almost like God designed night and day that way (Gen 1:3-5)! It seems he knew that our capacity here on Earth is limited, even if we have a "helper" (Gen 2:18).

Of course, the length of a day is significant because **work (or toil or activity) is a key part of our created purpose**, as we discovered in chapter 2. This is true because we know God is a worker, and we are made in his image.

---

13 If—as best-selling author John Gray suggested—men really are from Mars (which has a similar length day to Earth), and women are from Venus, that at least might explain why women seem to get so much more done.

God rests, so we rest

But God is not just a worker. He also rests:

> And on the seventh day God finished his work that
> he had done, and he rested on the seventh day from
> all his work that he had done. (Gen 2:2)

In resting, as with working, God sets a pattern for us who
bear his image. We see that weekly pattern clearly spelled
out when God provides his commandments to his people:

> "Remember the Sabbath day, to keep it holy. Six
> days you shall labour, and do all your work, but the
> seventh day is a Sabbath to the Lord your God. On
> it you shall not do any work, you, or your son, or
> your daughter, your male servant, or your female
> servant, or your livestock, or the sojourner who is
> within your gates." (Exod 20:8-10)

Why is that Sabbath pattern established by God? The very
next verse spells it out:

> "For in six days the Lord made heaven and earth,
> the sea, and all that is in them, and rested on the
> seventh day. Therefore the Lord blessed the Sab-
> bath day and made it holy." (Exod 20:11)

So God's pattern was to be our pattern, as we, his image-
bearers, reflect his nature.

What is the purpose of rest?

But I wonder if you have ever pondered this question: *why*
did God rest? Was he tired from all the hard work he had

done in creating the world?

Tiredness is an unlikely explanation, given God's unlimited power and the fact that he simply spoke the world into existence. The prophet Isaiah backs this up:

> Have you not known? Have you not heard?
> The LORD is the everlasting God,
>   the Creator of the ends of the earth.
> He does not faint or grow weary;
>   his understanding is unsearchable. (Isa 40:28)

God must have rested for some other reason.

I think we are meant to understand that God rests from his creative work in order to enjoy it and relate to it. He can enjoy it because "God saw everything that he had made" and he assessed it as "very good" (Gen 1:31). He sees that it is fit for his purpose—it's just the way he intended.

I get that. If I were a landscaper and had worked hard to create a beautiful garden which turned out exactly as I'd planned, I would take a break at the end of the final day of work, sit down with a nice cool drink in my hand, and enjoy the good thing I had made.

Indeed, that's the sort of image Genesis gives us in chapter 3 verse 8, when Adam and Eve hear "the sound of the LORD God walking in the garden in the cool of the day".

But in Genesis 3, it's not only a beautiful garden that God has created and is enjoying: he has created a man and a woman—people made in his image and with the ability to relate personally to him in a way unique among all of God's creations. God has not just paused his work to *enjoy* his creation's goodness. The fact that his presence is with

Adam and Eve in the garden is an indication that part of that enjoyment is found in personally *relating* to and *interacting* with his creation as its Creator.

I think I get that too. As a parent, when your baby is born you can only marvel at this new creation you and your spouse have made together. But for me, a lot of the real joy as a parent came as our children grew older and started to interact with us, then talk with us and snuggle up to us, and challenge us and argue with us (okay, not as much joy in that phase), and then in adulthood relate to us as close friends.

This relational dimension and other-person-centredness is fundamental to God's nature as three persons (Father, Son and Spirit). In the Trinity, God was a *relating* God even before he created the world. It's an intrinsic part of his very being.

And so our being, as those made in God's image, is also relational.[14]

In other words, **part of being image-bearers is having a special relationship with God that no other creatures are privileged to have**. Let that truth sink in for a moment, and then I suggest you pause and thank God for it![15]

That's why we can be sure our Sabbath rest is not intended purely for our physical benefit.

We tend to think of rest as *not* doing something (i.e. not doing our paid employment). But biblical rest involves more than that. It is pausing from our work and busyness

---

14 God says, "It is not good that the man should be alone" (Gen 2:18).
15 You might even like to go back and reflect again on Psalm 8 (see reflection question 2 in chapter 1).

to do something *different*.

Just as God rests to enjoy his relationship with his creation, we his creation pause from our work and busyness to take time to remember God and enjoy our relationship with him. God, in his enormous generosity, not only gives us created things (especially other people) to enjoy and relate to; he gives us the opportunity to enjoy and relate to him as our Creator.

Christians and the Sabbath

But we've skipped over an important question: Are we, as Christians, still under the Old Testament Sabbath law? Are we obligated to keep the command to rest on the seventh day?

A full answer to this question can have all sorts of nuances, but the bottom line is this: Jesus has fulfilled all the Old Testament law for us, and we're not judged on the basis of how well we keep those laws:

> "Do not think that I have come to abolish the Law or the Prophets; I have not come to abolish them but to fulfil them." (Matt 5:17)

> Therefore let no-one pass judgement on you in questions of food and drink, or with regard to a festival or a new moon or a Sabbath. These are a shadow of the things to come, but the substance belongs to Christ. (Col 2:16-17)

> For Christ is the end of the law for righteousness to everyone who believes. (Rom 10:4)

However, that doesn't mean we can't find guidance from the important principle that stands behind the Sabbath law and reflects the nature of our Creator himself. The clear principle is that it's good to take breaks from our work in order to be physically refreshed, remember God, rejoice in him, and focus our attention on engaging with him as our Creator.

That same principle is what Jesus reminds Martha about in the incident recorded for us in Luke 10:38-42.

There are two sisters, Mary and Martha, and they have Jesus visiting their home to teach.

Mary sits at Jesus' feet listening to him. Martha, meanwhile, is stressed and busy attending to the preparations that have to be made with such an important guest in the house. And, to be honest, Martha is a bit ticked off that Mary isn't helping. So she complains to Jesus. And Jesus says this:

> "Martha, Martha, you are anxious and troubled about many things, but one thing is necessary. Mary has chosen the good portion, which will not be taken away from her." (Luke 10:41-42)

Mary has turned aside from the household busyness to do something *better*. She is sitting at the feet of the Son of God worshipping him by listening to him.

The point is this: **while well-directed busyness is a good thing, there is more to life**. As good as they can be, work and busyness—and the material things that work and busyness offer us—are not the sum total of who we are as God's image-bearers. We need to draw aside from our work and busyness to rest and remember God, and engage with him as our Creator and rescuer (let's call this 'God rest').

My question for you is this: **Do you do that?** Do you have God rest? Do you, as an image-bearer of God, reflect that aspect of his nature and the way he has created us to both work *and* rest?

To what extent has life's busyness crowded out time for those key relationships with God and the people God has placed in your life?

Now that's not a hypothetical question. You'll see in the reflection section below that I want you to do something pretty outrageous—I want you to put an actual number on the time you spend in God rest.

And once you put a number on it, if your God rest quality or quantity seems low, do you think that might be a reason to do some reassessment and make some changes to your life?

Some additional thoughts about the nitty-gritty of 'God rest'

- Remembering God is a big theme in the Bible (and specifically connected to the Sabbath). One of the goals of 'God rest' is to focus our attention towards God and remember who he is and what he has done for us. God rest therefore ought to be marked by thankfulness for all the blessings he has given us (including our rescue in Christ) and by praise for his character and power.

- A big part of God rest happens through what Christians have generally called a 'quiet time'—a time set aside for reading the Bible, thanking and praising God, and praying to him (asking him for things). Many find it helpful to do that for half an hour or so at the same time each day so that it becomes a regular habit.

- There is also a corporate dimension to God rest, which is what we do when we gather together for small groups and for church, or when we read the Bible and pray with others (like our kids or spouse or a friend). We remember God *together*.

- Part of the Sabbath is that the day is 'holy' (Exod 20:8) or different/set apart. In other words, when we rest, it should probably look quite different to our non-rest time. So, for example, if much of your week is spent in front of screens, perhaps much of your God rest time is a time when screens are turned off. Or if your busyness involves being with people a lot, maybe God rest time involves having some 'alone' time when you can focus on you and God. Maybe reading a Christian book in your God rest time could be something helpful which you don't normally do.

- Many 'restful' activities—like, for example, going for a hike—can become God rest simply by expressing your thankfulness to God for this beautiful creation he has given you to enjoy and the people you are enjoying it with. It might be prayers like "God, that river you've made is so stunning. Thank you for blessing me with your creativity." Or using the time to pray for family and friends. Or suggesting to the person you are with, "Hey, as we walk, why don't we share three things about this last week that we are really thankful to the Lord for?" (And then stop your walk in a nice spot and express in prayer your thankfulness to God for those things.)

- Weekends away—on your own, with your family, or even with your church family—can be a really beneficial way of removing yourself from the normal activities of life and dwelling on God for an extended period. Could you do that a few times a year for a day or two?

- Kids' activities, like sports, can really add to our busyness and can certainly interfere with our God rest, especially on a Sunday. Is that an issue that needs addressing in the life of your family?[16]

---

16 You might find Todd Hill's article at *The Gospel Coalition* a helpful Christian perspective on kids and sport: 'Do Christian parents flirt with the idol of sports?', 24 February 2016 (thegospelcoalition.org/article/do-christian-parents-flirt-with-the-idol-of-sports). For more on the topic of sport and Christians, see *The Good Sporting Life: Loving and playing sport as a follower of Jesus* by Stephen Liggins. There's also more on the topic of family life and kids' activities in appendix 3 of this book.

Reflection

1. What proportion of your time each week could you reasonably categorize as the sort of 'God rest' that is described above? (Go on, be brave and put a number on it!) Does this adequately reflect God's work/rest pattern? If not, what stops you from taking more God rest? What can you do about it?

2. Read Psalm 92 (which is described as a psalm "for the Sabbath") a few times in this coming week. Try to align your heart with the psalmist's and make his words to God your own.

3. Read Matthew 14 and observe the demands on Jesus' time. Given those demands, why do you think he withdraws "to a desolate place by himself" (v 13)?

Chapter by chapter summary	
1	God is our Creator and we are made in his image. We are like him, but also different.
2	God works; he is busy. God gives us, his image-bearers, work to do. Work or busyness is a good thing if it is well-directed.
3	God doesn't just work;, he rests. God wants us, as his image-bearers, to rest too. Rest recognizes there is more to life than work and grants us time to enjoy God and all he gives us.
4	
5	
6	
7	
8	
9	
10	
11	

4.
God's metanarrative

At the end of chapter 2, we arrived at the conclusion that well-directed busyness is actually a good thing. And this was partly based on the truth that God is a worker and he made us in his likeness as workers.

But unless we figure out what we mean by "well-directed" busyness, that conclusion is about as useful as an inflatable dartboard.

So how do we do that?

The answer is found in recognizing that God has revealed in the Bible his metanarrative for our world, and our own narrative—our personal direction—is set according to that metanarrative.

"Wait—what the heck's a metanarrative?"

Good question! It's basically a fancy word for 'story'. But it's not just *any* story. A metanarrative is the big *overarching* story that provides the context for the smaller stories within it. The metanarrative shapes and gives context to the subnarratives.

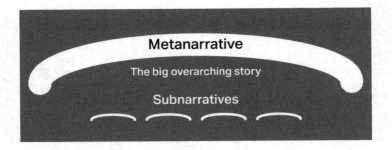

Metanarrative
The big overarching story
Subnarratives

So, for example, many years ago I read a book called *Forgiving Hitler*.[17] It tells the true story of a lady named Kathy Diosy. Kathy was a Hungarian Jew who lost many of her family members in the Holocaust. Yet she survived, emigrated to Australia, and many years later became a Christian.

Now Kathy's personal story has as its backdrop—its metanarrative—the bigger story of the rise of the Nazi regime and the war in Europe. The book isn't *about* that bigger story, but you can't understand her personal story without understanding that overarching story. If you knew nothing about the Holocaust, you would find Kathy's personal story hard to make sense of.

But above the story of 20th-century European history is an even bigger story, a more overarching story still ... and that is the story revealed in the Bible of what God is doing in our world.

God's metanarrative is, in one sense, a fairly linear and simple one: it goes from Point A in Genesis 1, which starts at creation and the words "In the beginning ...",

---

17 Sadly it's no longer in print. Hey, Matthias Media publishing department, if you're reading this, you should bring it back as an ebook.

and it heads towards Point B, which is the new creation described near the end of the last book of the Bible, in Revelation 21-22. From creation to new creation; Point A to Point B.

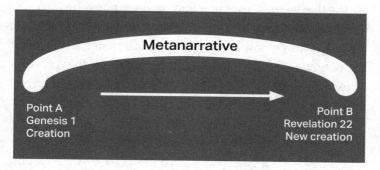

Of course, that's the high-level overview you can see from up in the helicopter.[18] Down on the ground, in the detail of the story, there are all sorts of twists and turns—even ultra-low points when it looks like Point B is never going to happen and maybe God has given up on bringing about the new creation. But God doesn't ever give up.[19] As we saw in chapter 2, he is all-powerful and he always achieves his plans and goals.

---

18 This high-level view is sometimes referred to as 'biblical theology'—that is, the study of how the whole Bible fits together as one story and points to Jesus Christ. To learn more: for newer Christians or non-Christians, I'd recommend *The Book of Books: A short guide to reading the Bible* by Geoff Robson; for more established Christians I'd suggest *Gospel and Kingdom: A Christian interpretation of the Old Testament* by Graeme Goldsworthy or *God's Big Picture: Tracing the storyline of the Bible* by Vaughan Roberts.

19 The problem is always the faithlessness of his people, not God. As Paul writes in 2 Timothy 2:13, "if we are faithless, he remains faithful—for he cannot deny himself".

Why does this matter? Well, because there is a through-line to history which gives all of us within that story a clear direction: we're part of God's story that moves from Point A to Point B.

It's like we're actors in a play, and we know how to act our part because we have read the ending of the play. If we didn't know how the play ended, we might struggle to know how to act throughout it. It would be like playing Romeo in Shakespeare's *Romeo and Juliet*, and completely hamming it up for laughs, not realizing the play ends in poignant tragedy.

In other words, our lives aren't random and direction-less. They have a goal and a purpose as part of God's big plan for the world. And that big plan gives us a direction for our lives and a frame of reference for making decisions about what's important.

Well-directed busyness

So when we say busyness is a good thing if our busyness is well-directed (chapter 2), you can no doubt see why God's metanarrative helps us work out what 'well-directed' means.

If the sovereign God, our Creator, has a big overarching purpose and direction for the world—and remember he always achieves what he sets out to achieve—then the least futile or best things we can do in this life are those that align with his purpose and his direction—with his metanarrative. Well-directed busyness is busyness that serves God's plan for Point B.

So what is that Point B like? What are we working

towards with God? God gives us a thrilling description of the new creation in Revelation 21:

> Then I saw a new heaven and a new earth, for the first heaven and the first earth had passed away ... And I heard a loud voice from the throne saying, "Behold the dwelling place of God is with man. He will dwell with them, and they will be his people, and God himself will be with them as their God. He will wipe every tear from their eyes, and death shall be no more, neither shall there be mourning, nor crying, nor pain anymore, for the former things have passed away." (Rev 21:1-4)

Point B is the kingdom of God, where Jesus is seated on his throne—the king above all kings—with every knee bowing to him as king and everything united under his rule:

> ... making known to us the mystery of his will, according to his purpose, which he set forth in Christ as a plan for the fullness of time, to unite all things in him, things in heaven and things on earth. (Eph 1:9-10)

> Therefore God has highly exalted him and bestowed on him the name that is above every name, so that at the name of Jesus every knee should bow, in heaven and on earth and under the earth, and every tongue confess that Jesus Christ is Lord, to the glory of God the Father. (Phil 2:9-11)

Interestingly, the Bible also describes Point B, the new creation or kingdom, as our 'rest' (Hebrews 4)—a time when the frustrations and sufferings of this world all come to an end and we will fully enjoy relationship with God, because the dwelling of God will be with his people and he will live with us and be our God:

> For if Joshua had given them rest [i.e. the Jews in the promised land], God would not have spoken of another day later on. So then, there remains a Sabbath rest for the people of God, for whoever has entered God's rest has also rested from his works as God did from his. (Heb 4:8-10)

Now the promised, perfect God rest that still awaits us at Point B doesn't necessarily involve an absence of any activity on our part—just as God resting from his work (Heb 4:10) doesn't mean *he* is no longer active in the world.[20] I *am*, however, very sure it means an end to the cursed *frustration* of any such activity, particularly the frustration that formerly happened because of our sinful rebellion against God. That rebellion comes to an end in the new creation, and with it, that frustration.

Furthermore, the activity God gave Adam and Eve was part of the 'good' in that first perfect creation; it was not a distraction from relating to God. Such activity is a blessing to us, so why would it not be part of the new creation as well?

---

20 I think the work God had finished is the work he needed to do to establish his kingdom in Jesus. That's why "after making purification for sins" Jesus "sat down" (Heb 1:3). Unlike the priests, who stand day after day offering sacrifices, Jesus offered a "single sacrifice" that was full and sufficient for all time (Heb 10:11-12).

But the main point of this chapter is this: God has planned a beginning and an end to history—to his story, his metanarrative—a beginning (Point A) and end (Point B) that give us purpose and direction for our lives.

That revelation is going to be super helpful to our thinking about well-directed busyness.

Reflection

1. Read 2 Peter 3:1-18. Even from the earliest days of the church, there were scoffers who asked: Where is this promised 'coming'? (In other words, where is this Point B? Surely you can't really believe in such a thing, let alone think it is coming soon!)

   a. What is Peter's answer to such scoffers?

   b. Do you have trouble believing/remembering that God has promised to bring an end to this creation and establish "new heavens and a new earth in which righteousness dwells" (v 13)? Why/why not?

   c. What does Peter say we should be or do in light of God's promise?

2. How much thought do you give to God's metanarrative? To what extent does it drive your daily activity and your prayers? Do you pray "Your kingdom come"?

Chapter by chapter summary	
1	God is our Creator and we are made in his image. We are like him, but also different.
2	God works; he is busy. God gives us, his image-bearers, work to do. Work or busyness is a good thing if it is well-directed.
3	God doesn't just work; he rests. God wants us, as his image-bearers, to rest too. Rest recognizes there is more to life than work and grants us time to enjoy God and all he gives us.
4	God has a plan, or a metanarrative, which shapes our own plan or narrative. His plan is revealed in the Bible and goes from Point A (creation) to Point B (new creation/God's kingdom).
5	
6	
7	
8	
9	
10	
11	

5.
The roadblock removed

In our previous chapter we saw that God has a plan that is heading towards Point B—the future new creation described in Revelation 21, the kingdom where Jesus is King, there is no ongoing rebellion, and everyone and everything submits to his rule. A sinless, painless, deathless, perfect place of fellowship with the living Creator God—it's our rest, with a capital 'R'. Our ultimate God rest.

But there's an obvious problem.

In his autobiography, *Groucho and Me*, the late, great comedian Groucho Marx recounts the time he sent a telegram to a club of which he was a member:

> PLEASE ACCEPT MY RESIGNATION. I DON'T WANT TO BELONG TO ANY CLUB THAT WILL ACCEPT PEOPLE LIKE ME AS A MEMBER.[21]

It's a bit like that with membership of Christ's kingdom: if it has people like me in it, I'm not sure I want to join! It

---

21 Groucho Marx, *Groucho and Me*, 4th edn, Da Capo Press, 1995, p 321.

certainly won't be a sinless and perfect kingdom if there are people like me as members.

The problem

And that's the issue: How can we be part of that sinless, perfect kingdom when we are definitely not sinless and perfect?[22]

> But nothing unclean will ever enter it, nor anyone who does what is detestable or false ... (Rev 21:27)

Here's the problem: we're in the heavenly courtroom, facing the judge (God) to see if he thinks we are suitable for this new kingdom. And we're faced with an imposing stack of evidence that all says we *shouldn't* be allowed in. The verdict should be 'Guilty—no access'.

> For all have sinned and fall short of the glory of God ... (Rom 3:23)

We are by nature children of God's wrath (Eph 2:3), not children of God's rest. So for us there's a massive sin road-block on the journey from Point A to Point B.

---

22 Sorry to interrupt. But this is one of those points I warned you about, where you might be feeling like we've strayed a long way from dealing with your busyness problems and your overly full diary. Like I said, please stick with me, because towards the end of the chapter we'll see that this heart of the Christian message—which you may be tempted to skip over because you've heard it before—has massive implications for how we think about ourselves and our busyness.

The solution

But, thanks be to God, he loved us, by sending his son Jesus into our world to remove that sin roadblock:

> Therefore, since we have been justified by faith, we have peace with God through our Lord Jesus Christ. Through him we have also obtained access by faith into this grace in which we stand, and we rejoice in hope of the glory of God. (Rom 5:1-2)

> But God, being rich in mercy, because of the great love with which he loved us, even when we were dead in our trespasses, made us alive together with Christ ... (Eph 2:4-5)

Indeed, Jesus is the whole reason for and substance of God's metanarrative: it's all about him—he is "the beginning and the end" (Rev 21:6, 22:13). He is also the *means* of achieving it: through his death and resurrection he provides the access to Point B, the entry to God's kingdom; Jesus is "the door" (John 10:1-18).

Why did God do all this?

> It was to show his righteousness at the present time, so that he might be just and the justifier of the one who has faith in Jesus. (Rom 3:26)

If God simply let us into his kingdom without dealing with our sin, that wouldn't be justice. It wouldn't be right. The Point A to Point B metanarrative without the cross of Christ as its central point would not reflect well on God's character.

Instead, God acts justly and deals with our sin through Jesus' death on the cross and his resurrection. And so he justifies those who have faith in God. In other words, for those who trust in Jesus the verdict has changed from:

guilty—no access

to:

not guilty—full and free access

There's now no barrier to entering into God's kingdom for those who have put their trust in Jesus.

From 'do' to 'done'

Do you remember that when Jesus was dying on the cross, and before he breathed his last breath, he said the remarkable words, "It is finished" (John 19:30)? His atoning work on the cross was done.

Because God has finished his saving work, there is nothing we can add to it in order to be saved. We don't need to work for our salvation. Indeed, we can't. We cannot justify ourselves. We simply rely on God justifying us through Jesus:

> Then they said to him, "What must we do, to be doing the works of God?" Jesus answered them, "This is the work of God, that you believe in him whom he has sent." (John 6:28-29)

That's a wonderful truth that has obvious relevance to our current and future relationship with God. We are reconciled now, and so will be saved in the future by Jesus:

> For if while we were enemies we were reconciled
> to God by the death of his Son, much more, now
> that we are reconciled, shall we be saved by his life.
> (Rom 5:10)

In fact, that future is so secure, the Bible speaks about Christians as people who have *already* been transferred to Point B—we have already 'checked in' to God's future kingdom. Look at how Paul puts it:

> He has delivered us from the domain of darkness
> and transferred us to the kingdom of his beloved
> Son, in whom we have redemption, the forgiveness
> of sins. (Col 1:13-14)

See the transfer that God accomplishes? He takes us from the domain of darkness[23] and transfers us into the kingdom of the Son whom he loves (Point B).

But note the *past tense* of the verbs: he *has* delivered us and transferred us. Not he *will* deliver us and transfer us.

We see a similar idea in Philippians:

> But our citizenship is in heaven, and from it we await
> a Saviour, the Lord Jesus Christ, who will transform
> our lowly body to be like his glorious body, by the
> power that enables him even to subject all things to
> himself. (Phil 3:20-21)

---

23 That is, having been removed from the garden in Genesis 3:23-24, mankind is now in this fallen, dark world of sin between Point A and Point B. More of this in the next chapter.

Again, note the present tense: our citizenship *is* in heaven (Point B), not it *will be* in heaven. Our citizenship has already been granted to us.

Paul must think this is significant, because he says it *again* in Ephesians:

> But God, being rich in mercy, because of the great love with which he loved us, even when we were dead in our trespasses, made us alive together with Christ—by grace you have been saved—and raised us up with him and seated us with him in the heavenly places in Christ Jesus, so that in the coming ages he might show the immeasurable riches of his grace in kindness towards us in Christ Jesus. (Eph 2:4-7)

See what God has *done*? He has "seated us with him [Christ] in the heavenly places". It's not that he is going to do it one day; for those who are in Christ it is already done.

Obviously, while all of this means we are spiritually at Point B, we are nonetheless still physically in this world: I'm still sitting at my computer writing this book; you're somewhere in this world reading it. Point B has not been fully achieved yet. God has chosen to leave us in this world for a time. And we'll think more about why in the next chapter.

Freed from slavery to busyness

The wonderful truth of our secure and guaranteed future is very liberating in terms of a lot of the busyness that consumes us.

You see, I don't have to prove my worth as a person to my dad, or to my boss,[24] or even to myself. That worth and significance comes instead from knowing that God was willing to pay the ultimate price to make me his child and give me an inheritance in his kingdom, his rest, his new creation.

My worth was already very significant simply by being part of God's good creation—the part of creation that God made in his image and chooses to bless and relate to. But my worth is absolutely secured by the acknowledgement of Jesus as my Lord:

> "Are not two sparrows sold for a penny? And not one of them will fall to the ground apart from your Father. But even the hairs of your head are all numbered. Fear not, therefore; you are of more value than many sparrows. So everyone who acknowledges me before men, I also will acknowledge before my Father who is in heaven, but whoever denies me before men, I also will deny before my Father who is in heaven." (Matt 10:29-33)

The acknowledgement of Jesus means we have received the privileged status of being children of God, and can now call God 'Abba, Father':

> See what kind of love the Father has given to us, that we should be called children of God; and so we are. (1 John 3:1)

---

24 I may have to justify my salary by doing good work that pleases my boss. But that's not the same as proving my intrinsic worth as a person.

For you did not receive the spirit of slavery to fall back into fear, but you have received the Spirit of adoption as sons, by whom we cry, "Abba! Father!" (Rom 8:15)

The word 'Abba' is an Aramaic term that experts find hard to translate into English. It has a sense of greater familiarity—a less formal form of address towards a father. Indeed, it is the name Jesus used in the garden of Gethsemane when praying his intimate prayer to his Father about his impending crucifixion (Mark 14:36). Can you believe that we can use the same form of address with God the Father as used by Jesus, his beloved son?

If there was ever any cloud of doubt over our worth in God's sight, it is blown away by Jesus' amazing, God-initiated act of love on the cross which facilitates our adoption.

So even if I achieve *nothing* in this world, I still can be sure that I am justified in God's sight by trusting in Jesus. **My worth in God's sight and my relationship with him is not dependent on my usefulness.**[25]

That last sentence contains such a countercultural, counterintuitive truth, I'm going to ask you to read it again: *My worth in God's sight and my relationship with him is not dependent on my usefulness.* I am not loved more

25 Think for example of the criminal on the cross next to Jesus (Luke 23:39-43). This criminal has done nothing to deserve God's rest, and has no more opportunities to earn it. Yet when he says, "Jesus, remember me when you come into your kingdom", Jesus replies with these wonderful words of assurance: "Truly, I say to you, today you will be with me in paradise".

by God when I am busy—even if the busyness involves gospel-driven Christian activities—and I am not loved less when I am not busy.

Earlier in the book I asked whether being a Christian is part of the busyness problem or the busyness solution. Superficially it looks like the former, but at a deep level, Jesus actually expects it to be the latter. His invitation is to those who are wearied from their labour and he promises rest and relief:

> "Come to me, all who labour and are heavy laden, and I will give you rest. Take my yoke upon you, and learn from me, for I am gentle and lowly in heart, and you will find rest for your souls. For my yoke is easy, and my burden is light." (Matt 11:28-30)[26]

And that rest ultimately comes from having a relationship with God the Father through Jesus the Son (Matt 11:25-27).

Like God's chosen people in the Old Testament, we don't have to strive to secure our blessed future:

> "Be still ['stop striving', NASB], and know that I am
> God.
> 　I will be exalted among the nations,
> 　I will be exalted in the earth!" (Ps 46:10)

For thus said the Lord GOD, the Holy One of Israel,
"In returning and rest you shall be saved;
　in quietness and in trust shall be your strength."
(Isa 30:15)

---

26 We will come back to this important verse later.

So stop striving as if it all depends on you. God is in charge. Know that he is God and he has it all under control. He will fulfil his plan for the new creation, Point B, and bring any opposition to his plan to an end. As his people, we can be sure that he's got our back.

That's not to say that our faithful, well-directed busyness is without any eternal significance. The New Testament makes it clear that "we must all appear before the judgement seat of Christ, so that each one may receive what is due for what he has done in the body, whether good or evil" (2 Cor 5:10). And the quality of our work will determine if it is "burned up" or if it will "receive a reward" (1 Cor 3:10-15).[27]

So while my usefulness is not what makes me valuable in God's sight, my well-directed busyness and work in this world is not pointless. It actually has great significance, as we will start to see in the next chapter.

YOLO?

The other thing this gospel truth frees us from is the dreadful tyranny of 'YOLO'. It stands for 'You Only Live Once', and it has become a bit of a slogan for our times. It's the idea that I should cram my life full of adventures

---

27 This idea of being rewarded in heaven for things we do in this life is tricky, and the New Testament really doesn't say a lot about it—perhaps because it could easily be misused to undermine our assurance of being justified by faith in Christ alone. Paul's words to the Thessalonians hints that the rewards are found in the recognition by Jesus of those we have served: "For what is our hope or joy or crown of boasting before our Lord Jesus at his coming? Is it not you? For you are our glory and joy" (1 Thess 2:19-20).

and experiences and fun—and of course strive for the financial success that pays for it all—because life is short and apparently you only get one go at it.

But because of the cross and resurrection of Jesus, YDOLO—You Don't Only Live Once. We can be absolutely sure that we have something more than this life to look forward to: Point B, the new creation. It offers everything good about this current creation, only far, far better.

In fact, although the apostle Paul loves his life of ministry and his service of God's people,[28] he knows that it pales in comparison to what awaits him in the new creation:

> For to me to live is Christ, and to die is gain. If I am to live in the flesh, that means fruitful labour for me. Yet which I shall choose I cannot tell. I am hard pressed between the two. My desire is to depart and be with Christ, for that is far better. (Phil 1:21-23)

Forget YOLO. What an awful, developed-world, self-indulgent and hollow philosophy of life that represents. If you don't think it's hollow, try reading Ecclesiastes. The guy who wrote that book did the full YOLO research project, and concluded it was all incredibly pointless:

> Whatever my eyes desired I did not keep from them. I kept my heart from no pleasure, for my heart found pleasure in all my toil, and this was my reward for all my toil. Then I considered all that my hands had done and the toil I had expended in doing it,

28 This is a way of thinking about life that we will come back to later.

and behold, all was vanity and a striving after wind, and there was nothing to be gained under the sun. (Eccl 2:10-11)

No, we have something much better to live by: a hope that is far more solid and which gives purpose to this life and a sure hope for a far better new life in the future.

Reflection

1. Have you personally put your trust in Jesus? How do your actions and thinking demonstrate that you are resting in his finished work for your salvation?

2. In what ways, and to what extent, is your busyness bound up with trying to justify yourself? To prove your worth? Or to cram everything into this earthly existence?

3. Has the YOLO philosophy influenced you and your friends? To what extent is the pursuit of pleasure an appropriate activity for a Christian?[29]

29 This is actually a really tricky question. In the context of the pleasures of marriage and food, the apostle Paul in 1 Timothy 4:4-5 reminds us that "everything created by God is good, and nothing is to be rejected if it is received with thanksgiving, for it is made holy by the word of God and prayer". So Christians are not ascetics. We can thankfully enjoy the pleasures of this world. But we're also not blind to the "vanity" of chasing pleasure. To think more deeply about this issue, I recommend Mikey Lynch's book *The Good Life in the Last Days: Making choices when the time is short*.

Chapter by chapter summary	
1	God is our Creator and we are made in his image. We are like him, but also different.
2	God works; he is busy. God gives us, his image-bearers, work to do. Work or busyness is a good thing if it is well-directed.
3	God doesn't just work; he rests. God wants us, as his image-bearers, to rest too. Rest recognizes there is more to life than work and grants us time to enjoy God and all he gives us.
4	God has a plan, or a metanarrative, which shapes our own plan or narrative. His plan is revealed in the Bible and goes from Point A (creation) to Point B (new creation/God's kingdom).
5	Our sin stops us from getting to Point B (God's kingdom), but Jesus has transferred us there already through his death and resurrection: guaranteed. Our worth is found not in our work or activity, but in Christ's.
6	
7	
8	
9	
10	
11	

6.
Where is God's metanarrative up to?

I'm going to share something that will make you think I'm old. Either that or you are so young that you'll have no idea what I'm talking about.

Here it is: up until fairly recently, I had a street directory in my car. Yes, I mean an *actual* book with maps printed using real ink on real paper.

Now, although the printed street directory had some advantages over these new-fangled GPS thingummies, it had one major fault: you had to know where you were in order to use it.[30]

Of course, knowing where you are is particularly important when you're trying to get somewhere specific. If you're happy just randomly meandering without any destination in mind, then it probably doesn't particularly matter where you are. (At least until you decide you want to head home.)

---

30 This required us to actually use our brains, looking out the car windows for clues like street signs or landmarks, and then trying to find those on the map.

In terms of God's metanarrative route from Point A to Point B, it can be very helpful to know where we are on the map. Remember, this is not because of any doubt about us getting there—we saw in the previous chapter that by trusting in Jesus our arrival at the destination is guaranteed. No, it's more that knowing where we are on the journey helps us to know what to do along the way.

So where are we?

As we saw in chapter 5, we are in one sense already at Point B. We have been transferred there in Christ. But we also noted the obvious point that we are not physically there yet; we still live in this current world.

So we're still joyfully looking forward to the complete fulfilment of the promise of the new creation at Point B. We do that not just because it is so certain, but because it's such a brilliant future to have ahead of us. (Remember the description from Revelation 21 we read back in chapter 4?) Jesus describes that future in one of his parables:

> The kingdom of heaven is like treasure hidden in a field, which a man found and covered up. Then in his joy he goes and sells all that he has and buys that field. (Matt 13:44)

The point Jesus is making is this: the promised kingdom of heaven is such a wonderful prospect that you'd willingly give up everything for it. All else in your life pales in comparison with this superb treasure that lies ahead of you. And the longing to take possession of it absolutely turns your life upside down. It is what you now live for!

Is that true for you? Because Jesus is saying that's how radical he expects the response of his followers to be to what he is offering. You might need to pause your reading for a while and honestly reflect on how much joy the idea of your future with God in his eternal kingdom gives you and how much it shapes your life choices.

Whilst we're not at Point B yet, neither are we still at Point A any longer. We're not living in the garden of Eden—we (i.e. Adam and Eve as our forebears) were removed from there by God. We're now living between Point A and Point B—in a fallen world that is under God's curse (Gen 3:14-24).

The Bible describes the current creation we are in as subject to corruption, in darkness, and groaning under God's judgement of sin:

> For I consider that the sufferings of this present time are not worth comparing with the glory that is to be revealed to us. For the creation waits with eager longing for the revealing of the sons of God. For the creation was subjected to futility, not willingly, but because of him who subjected it, in hope that the creation itself will be set free from its bondage to corruption and obtain the freedom of the glory of the children of God. For we know that the whole creation has been groaning together in the pains of childbirth until now. And not only the creation, but we ourselves, who have the firstfruits of the Spirit, groan inwardly as we wait eagerly for adoption as sons, the redemption of our bodies. (Rom 8:18-23)

So although we can look forward to a future 'glory'—an eagerly awaited treasure—while we wait we endure a world that groans with suffering because of the impact of sin.

Paul's choice of "childbirth" is a very apt metaphor for this experience. There is pain and suffering in childbirth, but at the end there is the joy of a baby being born and held in a parent's loving arms. In this current phase we experience short-term pain, but when we arrive at Point B we experience prolonged joy.

Our world continues to reject God and "suppress the truth" about him (Rom 1:18), and so God gives people up (vv 24, 26, 28) to their own evil. That's why there is suffering and groaning in our world in this present age of darkness.[31]

Light in the darkness

But here's the thing: as people become Christians and submit to Jesus as their king, the light of the future kingdom leaks back into the 'present age of darkness' phase of God's metanarrative.

---

31 By the way, this is another one of those points where you might be wondering what the connection to the topic of busyness is. But knowing where we are on the journey, and understanding the environment we are currently in, is vital to knowing how to act and what to prioritize.

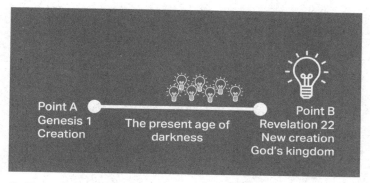

So Point B is where everyone submits to Jesus as the King, and that's why it is so *good*.

But in this current world, when people become Christians, they start submitting to Jesus as their King *now* (imperfectly, no doubt, but sincerely). In that sense there are little outbreaks of Jesus' kingdom popping up all over the place as people become Christians and live accordingly.

Although the future kingdom will be complete one day, in this present age it's a kingdom that is spreading like yeast through flour (Matt 13:33) or like a tiny seed that grows to become a big tree:

> "The kingdom of heaven is like a grain of mustard seed that a man took and sowed in his field. It is the smallest of all seeds, but when it has grown it is larger than all the garden plants and becomes a tree, so that the birds of the air come and make nests in its branches." (Matt 13:31-32)

In fact, we are part of the process of the kingdom spreading because our current lives are a light for our world

(Matt 5:14); they are evidence—in both word and deed—of the fact that Jesus is the great king. As Christians we are a living testimony to the joy of having found that great treasure—eternal reconciliation with God—that is of more worth to us than anything else in our lives.

Which, if you remember back to chapter 3, is exactly the truth of which the Sabbath is a weekly reminder. When I pause from my work to have 'God rest', I testify to myself and to others that my toil or work or activity of any sort is not the most important thing in my life. God is.

Living with great expectations

So we're living in the gap between Point A and Point B. And even as you read this book, that gap is growing chronologically bigger and bigger.

God created the world a long time ago. We won't get into a fiery debate as to exactly how long ago, but I think we can all agree that from a human perspective it's a good while.

And even if you calculate from the more recent date on which God sent his Son into the world to provide the means for us getting to Point B, it's been a while. Roughly 2000 years.

There's a reason for that long gap, of course. God tells us through the apostle Peter:

> But do not overlook this one fact, beloved, that with the Lord one day is as a thousand years, and a thousand years as one day. The Lord is not slow to fulfil his promise as some count slowness, but is patient

towards you, not wishing that any should perish, but that all should reach repentance. (2 Pet 3:8-9)

Judgement on sinners is God's "strange work", his "alien work" (Isa 28:21). God finds "no pleasure in the death of the wicked", but prefers "that the wicked turn from his way and live" (Ezek 33:11). It should come as no surprise, therefore, that God is delaying his judgement and giving those who are perishing more time.

The problem for us with that gap extending out for so many years now is that we can be lulled into complacency, which Peter goes on to address:

But the day of the Lord will come like a thief, and then the heavens will pass away with a roar, and the heavenly bodies will be burned up and dissolved, and the earth and the works that are done on it will be exposed. (2 Pet 3:10)

Surprisingly, this time we're spending in the gap could come to an end tonight. Just as thieves arrive unexpectedly, Jesus' arrival to bring an end to this present age of darkness could happen at any time. God may well be on the verge of drawing his metanarrative for the current world to a close. He may be about to bring in the new creation and deliver us to Point B.

If it's true that God might do that anytime, how should we respond? Peter again:

Since all these things are thus to be dissolved, what sort of people ought you to be in lives of holiness and godliness, waiting for and hastening the coming of the day of God, because of which the heavens will be set on fire and dissolved, and the heavenly bodies will melt as they burn! But according to his promise we are waiting for new heavens and a new earth in which righteousness dwells. (2 Pet 3:11-13)

So we know where we are on the map, and Peter is telling us about the appropriate way to act at this point in the journey. He's giving some detail about what 'well-directed busyness' looks like, given our great expectations for the future.

First of all, we ought to be *holy and godly*—people who are starting to take on the appearance of those who would rightly fit into a new creation "in which righteousness dwells". So as well as being transferred, we also need our character to be transformed.

Secondly, we *wait* for that new creation to arrive, in God's timing.

That might sound very passive and as if it has nothing to do with busyness. But what's the essence of waiting? *Remembering* what we are waiting for! And the older I get, the more I need to *do* things that help me not to forget!

The treasure of the kingdom is too valuable to risk forgetting about it. We mustn't treat the kingdom treasure like lots of Australian citizens apparently treat their bank accounts. At the moment the Australian government is holding around $1.2 billion in accounts that people have forgotten they have—amounts of up to $1 million for some people.

So a vital part of waiting is actively taking steps to

remember what belongs to you in Christ.

Thirdly, we don't just wait for it—Peter says we should *hasten its coming*.

So how do we do all that?

Read on. The rubber is about to start hitting the road.

Reflection

1. What evidence could you cite that the treasure of the kingdom of God has turned your life upside down? In what ways does your life testify to the truth that you live for something more than the things of this world?

2. Practically speaking, how do you keep the future treasure 'front of mind'?

3. In what ways do you think you have already been transformed to be more ready for the place where righteousness dwells? (Maybe ask someone who has known you well for some time. It can be hard to notice our own progress in holiness.)

4. What are some areas of your life in which you know you still need more transformation to happen?

Chapter by chapter summary	
1	God is our Creator and we are made in his image. We are like him, but also different.
2	God works; he is busy. God gives us, his image-bearers, work to do. Work or busyness is a good thing if it is well-directed.
3	God doesn't just work; he rests. God wants us, as his image-bearers, to rest too. Rest recognizes there is more to life than work and grants us time to enjoy God and all he gives us.
4	God has a plan, or a metanarrative, which shapes our own plan or narrative. His plan is revealed in the Bible and goes from Point A (creation) to Point B (new creation/God's kingdom).
5	Our sin stops us from getting to Point B (God's kingdom), but Jesus has transferred us there already through his death and resurrection: guaranteed. Our worth is found not in our work or activity, but in Christ's.
6	We now wait for the fulfilment of Point B—which could happen any day—being transformed day-by-day, ready for the future home of righteousness.
7	
8	
9	
10	
11	

7.
How to hasten the day

At my stage of life I don't particularly look forward to my birthday. It represents yet another digit being added to my age, and it's the annual event of looking and feeling awkward while people sing "Happy birthday to you".

But I can remember that birthdays felt very different as a kid. I longed to be a year older, and I couldn't wait to open my presents. In fact, the anticipation of an upcoming birthday was almost unbearable. Time simply could not pass quickly enough. I just wished I could make it come sooner.

Remember the parable of the treasure hidden in a field from our last chapter?

Do you think the man who reburied the treasure was more like me as a kid or me as a grumpy old man?

The whole point of the parable is that the man was extremely excited and couldn't wait to buy the field—to the extent that he did something pretty rash by selling all he owned to make that purchase as soon as he could. He 'hastened the day'.

And as we saw in the previous chapter, to 'hasten the

day' is one of the things the apostle Peter tells us we should do as we wait for the complete fulfilment of God's plan to deliver us to Point B.

But what does he mean? The answer is in the context. Let's look again at what Peter says:

> The Lord is not slow to fulfil his promise as some count slowness, but is patient toward you, not wishing that any should perish, but that all should reach repentance. (2 Pet 3:9)

So what is causing the delay in getting to Point B? It is the Lord intentionally delaying, out of patience, because he does not wish any to perish, but rather that all should reach repentance. And what is so important about repentance?

Firstly, it is the point at which the roadblock on the path to Point B is removed for the individual who is repenting and putting their faith in Christ. In other words, God is giving people more chance to be spiritually transferred to Point B through becoming Christians.

But secondly, repentance is also how we are transformed to be more ready for Point B. God is giving us more time to be transformed, and that transformation keeps us firmly on the path to Point B and away from the path of the perishing.

So what will hasten the day?

Answer: more people becoming Christians and every Christian being transformed more and more to be holy and godly. That's what God is waiting for. He is allowing more time for the kingdom of God to spread like yeast through dough (Matt 13:33).

So how should we live in light of this?

With the help of God's Spirit we can keep working on *our own* personal repentance and transformation as Christians. God's kingdom needs to spread *within us* as we each submit to Jesus as King more and more. Paul urges us to "work out your own salvation with fear and trembling, for it is God who works in you, both to will and to work for his good pleasure" (Phil 2:12-13). But part of being transformed as a Christian is to understand it's not all about me! I can also help *others* with their repentance, so that they also might be transferred and then be transformed as they wait for God to complete the journey to Point B. That's the way the kingdom yeast spreads. It's the way we are the light of the world. It's the way to hasten the day.

So while seeking the kingdom needs to *start* with you, the commandment to love your neighbour means it certainly shouldn't *end* with you. If you care about others, you'll want them to be part of Jesus' kingdom as well— you'll want them to be part of the new creation with you. You'll want to help them get to Point B too.

This type of love for others is something we noticed in passing in chapter 5, when we looked at the apostle Paul's comments in his letter to the Philippians—powerful comments on the meaning of his life and what he was looking forward to about his death.

The apostle's dilemma

Paul was asking himself a tough question in Philippians 1: Which is better—life or death? And he actually says it's hard to choose:

> It is my eager expectation and hope that I will not
> be at all ashamed, but that with full courage now as
> always Christ will be honoured in my body, whether
> by life or by death. For to me to live is Christ, and
> to die is gain. If I am to live in the flesh, that means
> fruitful labour for me. Yet which I shall choose I
> cannot tell. I am hard pressed between the two. My
> desire is to depart and be with Christ, for that is far
> better. But to remain in the flesh is more necessary
> on your account. Convinced of this, I know that
> I will remain and continue with you all, for your
> progress and joy in the faith, so that in me you may
> have ample cause to glory in Christ Jesus, because
> of my coming to you again. (Phil 1:20-26)

It's hard to choose because "to live is Christ, and to die is gain". Two good options.

As Christians we can surely understand why death is "gain", even if we struggle with an ongoing fear of dying. Death means finally arriving at Point B—the paradise of being with Christ in heaven.

But what does Paul say about what makes his *life* worthwhile? What does he mean when he says "to live is Christ"?

Fortunately, we don't have to guess—he provides the answer.

To go on living, he says, means "fruitful labour". He's not wasting his time just waiting for Jesus' kingdom to finally arrive or his own death to happen. No, he regards his busyness (labour) as very worthwhile (fruitful); he perceives it as having such a high value that it gives him a prime reason to go on living.

What gives his life such value? Living means he can continue to do the work that is for the "progress and joy in the faith" of the Philippians, so that they will also "glory in Christ Jesus".

That's what Paul says adds real value to his life: to help others progress and have joy in the faith. Life is about seeing others come to know the joy of being saved by the Lord Jesus, then urging and helping them to make progress towards maturity in their faith and so arrive safely at Point B. That is Paul's idea of 'well-directed busyness'.

Paul is happy to have his departure for Point B delayed, because he realizes he can help many others around him to get there too.

I once heard the story—perhaps apocryphal—of a man interviewed for a senior executive position. For the first part of the process the interviewer softens the executive up and gets him all nice and relaxed by asking some pretty friendly and easy questions. Then, out of the blue, he hits him with the big question—expecting the executive, like so many executives before him, to be a bit flustered by it.

"What's your ultimate goal in life?" asks the interviewer. Quick as a flash the executive says, "My goal is to be ready for heaven and to take as many people with me as possible."

It's the interviewer who ends up flustered and not sure what to say!

But that's it, isn't it? That's the goal the apostle Paul has. It's the goal we can have in life that genuinely aligns with God's metanarrative.

When Jesus returns, or we die and go to be with him,

we want to be one of his forgiven people, living faithfully for him as our king, and helping other people to also find forgiveness and live with Jesus as their king. Together we now live as members of his kingdom, standing ready to fully and finally enter his kingdom when God chooses to bring an end to this current world's metanarrative.[32] Nothing glorifies Jesus more than that. That's why Jesus taught his disciples to pray "your kingdom come".

That's the goal. But what's the means?

So as we continue exploring the topic of busyness and what 'well-directed busyness' might look like, let's consider how people find forgiveness and live with Jesus as their king. What's involved? How do we help them from Point A to Point B?

We can summarize it with four Ps:

People
Proclamation
Prayer
Perseverance[33]

God uses people: There may be other ways he could make and grow disciples of Jesus, but at the end of Matthew's Gospel Jesus chooses to commission people like you and me to do it:

---

32 Of course, God's full metanarrative doesn't have an end, because God has no end and his kingdom is eternal.

33 I'm indebted to my two friends Tony Payne and Colin Marshall for the clear articulation of these four Ps in their book *The Vine Project: Shaping your ministry culture around disciple-making.*

"All authority in heaven and on earth has been given to me. Go therefore and make disciples of all nations, baptizing them in the name of the Father and of the Son and of the Holy Spirit, teaching them to observe all that I have commanded you. And behold, I am with you always, to the end of the age." (Matt 28:18-20)

God uses proclamation: God uses people like you and me testifying to and teaching others what God has done for us in Jesus and teaching them to observe all that Jesus has commanded them. This involves reading God's word, the Bible, with them, explaining it, and living it out in front of them. It's sharing God's word with them in whatever ways we can: in a letter or email or SMS, chatting over the back fence, encouraging them at church or home group, doing cold-turkey evangelism,[34] sharing a Christian book, singing ... and in a thousand or more other ways.[35] The different ways we can use to bring God's word to people are only limited by our imagination and creativity.

God uses prayer: In the end, it is only as God works in people's hearts and minds through his Holy Spirit that they come to faith in Jesus. "The god of this world has blinded the minds of the unbelievers, to keep them from seeing the light of the gospel of the glory of Christ" (2 Cor 4:4). But by God's grace ...

---

34 Cold-turkey evangelism involves walking up to strangers in the street or shopping mall and attempting to talk to them about the gospel of Jesus.
35 For more on how to do this, see *Encouragement: How words change lives* by Gordon Cheng.

> ... when one turns to the Lord, the veil is removed. Now the Lord is the Spirit, and where the Spirit of the Lord is, there is freedom. (2 Cor 3:16-17)

So we beg God to take away that blindness and bring gospel freedom to people by his Spirit working in them.

But it doesn't stop when they become Christians; we continue to pray, not only for their joy, but also for their ongoing progress. Epaphras is a great example:

> Epaphras, who is one of you, a servant of Christ Jesus, greets you, always struggling on your behalf in his prayers, that you may stand mature and fully assured in all the will of God. (Col 4:12)

God uses perseverance: Although when people come to faith they are instantly transferred from the domain of darkness into the kingdom of God's beloved Son (Col 1:13), people are not instantly transformed into those who are fit for that kingdom. Like us, they become a work in progress. Paul points out that once the veil is removed, there is an ongoing transformation:

> And we all, with unveiled face, beholding the glory of the Lord, are being transformed into the same image from one degree of glory to another. For this comes from the Lord who is the Spirit. (2 Cor 3:18)

In other words, we don't give up on people when their transfer or transformation seems to us to be painfully slow. We persevere.

● ● ●

That's how God's kingdom is grown: by people expressing their love for others through prayerful proclamation that lovingly perseveres over time.

That's effectively what Paul has in mind in 1 Corinthians 15:58:

> Therefore, my beloved brothers, be steadfast, immovable, always abounding in the work of the Lord, knowing that in the Lord your labour is not in vain.

Since Jesus has conquered death through his resurrection, there is a form of busyness that is not "in vain". It's not in vain because it is aligned with the metanarrative God is totally committed to implementing—it is literally therefore "the work of the Lord". This work of the Lord can't be frustrated or undone by the fallen and temporary nature of this world.

This is the work we should abound in, or, as the NIV puts it, "give yourselves fully to". All our activity can be done "as for the Lord" (Col 3:23); but there is a category of activity that is specifically "the work of the Lord", because it involves those four Ps that God uses to transfer and transform people.[36]

---

36 For a fuller discussion of "the work of the Lord" in 1 Corinthians 15:58, see Peter Orr's *Briefing* article 'The work of the Lord', 2 September 2014 (thebriefing.com.au/2014/09/the-work-of-the-lord); or his longer and even more detailed article on the same topic in *Themelios*, 'Abounding in the work of the Lord (1 Cor 15:58): Everything we do as Christians or specific gospel work?', 13 August 2013 (thegospelcoalition.org/themelios/article/abounding-in-the-work-of-the-lord-1-cor-1558-everything-we-do-as-christians).

Remember the urgency

Having gained some clarity about the task, I want to briefly come back to remind us of the urgency.

In chapter 6 we saw from 2 Peter 3:10 that the coming of the new creation and our arrival at Point B could happen anytime—it will come like a thief in the night.[37]

And so there is an urgency and priority to the commission we have been given. It's described as the spiritual battle in which we are soldiers (Eph 6:11-13; Phil 2:25; 2 Tim 2:3).

I've never been in a real-life battle; but I imagine it does tend to focus the mind.

As you engage in fierce combat, I can't imagine you're wondering if you remembered to turn the stove off before you left home! No, the seriousness of the battle demands your utmost attention.

A good soldier, says Paul, doesn't get "entangled in civilian pursuits, since his aim is to please the one who enlisted him" (2 Tim 2:4). He is like a dedicated "athlete" (v 5) or "hard-working farmer" (v 6).[38]

So the battle is on, and the urgency of the work of hastening the coming of the day of God is high. Focusing on well-directed busyness is the order of the day.

To emphasize the point, Paul uses a bit of what I suspect is hyperbole in 1 Corinthians 7. Ideally, he says,

---

37 No doubt Peter gained this awareness from Jesus (see Matt 24:42-44).
38 That is, the farmer who feels fatigued from his labour. This is another example of how positive the Bible often is about working hard in worthwhile pursuits.

the married man would live as if he wasn't even married:[39]

> This is what I mean, brothers: the appointed time has grown very short. From now on, let those who have wives live as though they had none, and those who mourn as though they were not mourning, and those who rejoice as though they were not rejoicing, and those who buy as though they had no goods, and those who deal with the world as though they had no dealings with it. For the present form of this world is passing away. (1 Cor 7:29-31)

Knowing that the time is short, knowing that "the present form of this world is passing away"—potentially very soon; we don't know—we ought to hold on to the material things of this world very lightly. They aren't the things to show devotion to—Jesus is (1 Cor 7:35).

Now is not the time to drift along aimlessly. Rather, fight in the battle for souls.

Make yourself busy—'well-directed busy'—by abounding in the work of the Lord.

But ... please don't forget to rest.[40]

---

39 I suspect hyperbole because he has only just talked about the importance of married people doing married things (1 Cor 7:3-5) and not separating from each other (vv 10-11). And we know from passages like Ephesians 5:25-33 that husbands are to love their wives. I've seen men treating their wives as if they don't exist, and it's not loving!

40 Chapter 3!

Reflection

1. Has the delay in Jesus' return lulled you into a sense that evangelism and disciple-making is not urgent? If so, how can you develop a greater sense of urgency?

2. What specifically are you doing in your weekly routine which hastens the coming of the day of God?

3. Read Jesus' parable of the talents in Matthew 25:14-30. Given all the resources God has given you (time, money, education, access to the Scriptures, a good church, etc.), are you giving him a good return on his investment? Will God say to you "Well done, good and faithful servant" (vv 21, 23)? Or might he conclude that you have been a "wicked and slothful servant" (v 26)? Why?

4. Have you ever considered gospel work as a full-time job (e.g. as a pastor or missionary)? If not, why not? If so, what would it look like for you and how would you get there from where you are now?[41]

---

41 Let me commend the Ministry Training Strategy organization to you if you are considering the option of full-time paid ministry (mts.com.au).

Chapter by chapter summary	
1	God is our Creator and we are made in his image. We are like him, but also different.
2	God works; he is busy. God gives us, his image-bearers, work to do. Work or busyness is a good thing if it is well-directed.
3	God doesn't just work; he rests. God wants us, as his image-bearers, to rest too. Rest recognizes there is more to life than work and grants us time to enjoy God and all he gives us.
4	God has a plan, or a metanarrative, which shapes our own plan or narrative. His plan is revealed in the Bible and goes from Point A (creation) to Point B (new creation/God's kingdom).
5	Our sin stops us from getting to Point B (God's kingdom), but Jesus has transferred us there already through his death and resurrection: guaranteed. Our worth is found not in our work or activity, but in Christ's.
6	We now wait for the fulfilment of Point B—which could happen any day—being transformed day-by-day, ready for the future home of righteousness.
7	God is patiently waiting for more people to repent and be ready for the day of Point B. So we hasten that day by "abounding in the work of the Lord"—helping people to be transferred and then transformed as they wait.
8	
9	
10	
11	

8.
Waiting and hastening together

So we have found some really well-directed busyness to commit to in chapter 7—busyness that lines up well with God's plan for the world.

But, as we start to get a bit more into the practical end of this book, it's important for us to remember something we noted way back in chapter 1: in this world there is a category of 'all-powerful God'—and you and me, we're not in that category. We're not God. Unlike him, our time, energy, emotions and other resources are all limited. As one of my pastor friends sometimes says to people he fears are close to burning out: "There's only one saviour of the world, and it's not you!"

That's why the last sentence of our previous chapter—all about what we can be doing to hasten the day—was "But ... please don't forget to rest".

The Old Testament's weekly Sabbath was a regular reminder of the need to do that. But it was also a reminder of another important principle for God's people.

The corporate Sabbath

Even from those very first days of God's Old Testament people there was a very significant corporate dimension to the weekly reminder:

> "There are six days when you may work, but the seventh day is a Sabbath of rest, a day of sacred assembly." (Lev 23:3, NIV)[42]

The Sabbath was not a day when the Israelites all stayed at home and did no work privately, on their own. No, they *got together* and did no work. They had a day of "sacred assembly". And in so doing they showed all the other nations that this nation of God's people was very different. This nation had something more. This nation had a relationship with the living God!

Church

In an important way, it's still the same today for us as Christians. When we, as God's people, stop our work, draw aside from our busyness, and get together on a Sunday at church (or midweek in our small groups), we are doing at least three important things.

Firstly, we are going back to that field together, digging up our treasure, and reminding each other how totally brilliant it is. We take a little peek and we rekindle that desire to one day permanently hold that treasure in our hands.

---

42 I've used the NIV translation for this verse. The ESV, for some reason, uses the word 'convocation' instead of 'assembly'. I, for one, had no idea what 'convocation' meant.

In other words, we meet to remind one another just what we are waiting for, and encourage each other to be transferred and transformed in anticipation of Point B. That is, we wait in holiness and godliness *together*.

Secondly, we join up to act as one body—all playing our part and using our different gifts (see 1 Corinthians 12). We are not engaging in a solo sport when we 'hasten the day'; it's a team sport. And, as the saying goes, the whole is greater than the sum of the parts. We can achieve more 'kingdom spread' by working in partnership with each other.

And thirdly, like Israel did, we are testifying to the nations. The very act of us gathering together testifies to those around us that we live for something more than work, or sport, or our garden, or our house, or even our families. Our kingdom light shines out in the darkness, pointing people to something more—just like the word 'Eternity' being lit up on the Sydney Harbour Bridge.[43]

When we, for example, talk to other parents and tell them that we can't come to their child's birthday party on a Sunday morning—because we want to keep our family commitment to church—they may be a little disappointed, but deep down they'll hopefully see that we have something important in our lives.[44] And we pray that God

---

43 See the photo and find out the story behind it: K Patoway, 'The story behind Sydney's "Eternity" graffiti', *Amusing Planet*, 20 July 2018 (amusing planet.com/2018/07/the-story-behind-sydneys-eternity.html).

44 Of course, how much of a testimony it is might depend on how you explain it. "Sorry, Joey can't come to the party because we have to go to church" might be less of a positive witness than "Sorry, Joey can't come to the party. Sunday morning church is central to our family's week because Jesus is central to our family life. Perhaps the kids could catch up some other time in the week?"

will use that testimony to point them to his Son Jesus.

There's a similar idea in Paul's letter to the Ephesians when he points out that even Gentiles have now been shown God's grace (Eph 3:8) and been counted as God's people (i.e. part of his church). So Paul says that "through the church the manifold wisdom of God might now be made known to the rulers and authorities in the heavenly places" (Eph 3:10). In other words, when Jews and Gentiles unite in church, God is putting on public display the glorious reality that his kingdom is for both Jews and Gentiles.

When we show up for church, we make known in this darkened age the amazing unity in diversity that God has created, that will one day be carried into the new creation:

> After this I looked, and behold, a great multitude that no-one could number, from every nation, from all tribes and peoples and languages, standing before the throne and before the Lamb, clothed in white robes, with palm branches in their hands, and crying out with a loud voice, "Salvation belongs to our God who sits on the throne, and to the Lamb!" (Rev 7:9-10)

Church now is a foretaste of that future heavenly assembly. And so your presence in church helps demonstrate that unity and that the treasure of the kingdom (Point B) is not just for men, it's for women too. It's not just for Australians, it's for all ethnicities. It's not just for old people, it's for young people. It's not just for married people, it's for single people. It's not just for the able, but for those with a disability.

Our diversity in church manifests the fact that God's grace now extends to all types and categories of people. That's one of the many reasons you being in church makes a tangible difference.

But it's not only a witness to the outside world. As I said earlier, when we gather for church, we testify to each other and remind each other of the treasure we have found, and we urge each other to keep pursuing that treasure.

By just turning up—before you even open your mouth to sing or pray or read the Bible or preach or chat—you are testifying by your very presence at church that you think there is to be found in Christ a treasure that is worth giving up your Sunday morning for (and more). That encourages the other people joining you at church to keep remembering and living for God's metanarrative too.

In fact, for all of these reasons and more, I want to suggest to you that meeting together every week with other Christians, whether at church or in a home group or one-to-one, is vitally important. It is probably one of the most significant things you do regularly each week, if not *the* most.

The writer to Hebrews seems to agree:

> Let us hold fast the confession of our hope without wavering, for he who promised is faithful. And let us consider how to stir up one another to love and good works, not neglecting to meet together, as is the habit of some, but encouraging one another, and all the more as you see the Day drawing near. (Heb 10:23-25)

So here's the bottom line for this chapter: as a current transferee into Point B, if you're too busy to meet with other Christians on a consistently regular basis, you're definitely too busy. Something needs to change.

Reflection

1. How committed are you to church? Or to your home Bible study group? What is the evidence for your answer?[45]

2. Read Hebrews 10:24-25. The writer tells us not to neglect meeting together.

   a. Why? What will we miss out on if we do?

   b. Why should we do these things "all the more as you see the Day drawing near"?

3. Is going to church meant to be 'busyness' or 'rest'? Why? Are those two things at odds? If so, why? If not, why not?

---

45 It can be quite difficult to objectively assess our own commitment to church. For a start, we tend to overlook how often we've been absent. So if you're brave, why not ask your pastor or group leader how committed they think you are? I suspect you even asking the question will be an encouragement.

Chapter by chapter summary	
1	God is our Creator and we are made in his image. We are like him, but also different.
2	God works; he is busy. God gives us, his image-bearers, work to do. Work or busyness is a good thing if it is well-directed.
3	God doesn't just work; he rests. God wants us, as his image-bearers, to rest too. Rest recognizes there is more to life than work and grants us time to enjoy God and all he gives us.
4	God has a plan, or a metanarrative, which shapes our own plan or narrative. His plan is revealed in the Bible and goes from Point A (creation) to Point B (new creation/God's kingdom).
5	Our sin stops us from getting to Point B (God's kingdom), but Jesus has transferred us there already through his death and resurrection: guaranteed. Our worth is found not in our work or activity, but in Christ's.
6	We now wait for the fulfilment of Point B—which could happen any day—being transformed day-by-day, ready for the future home of righteousness.
7	God is patiently waiting for more people to repent and be ready for the day of Point B. So we hasten that day by "abounding in the work of the Lord"—helping people to be transferred and then transformed as they wait.
8	We wait together—as the church—encouraging each other and testifying to our world together. In God's meta-narrative, the church is crucial; so it will also be top priority in our well-directed lives.
9	
10	
11	

9.
Intentional relationships

Let's recap.

There's nothing wrong with being busy. But that statement comes with two qualifications.

Firstly, the busyness we should be aiming for is *well-directed* busyness. And we now know what well-directed busyness is about: it's about the journey to Point B, and the people God is giving us time to grab onto and bring with us.[46]

Secondly, we need rest. More than just rest—we need, and ought to have, God rest.

Not only do we need rest, most of us have secular jobs that we have to hold down, and perhaps other responsibilities we can't—often shouldn't—neglect.

So given the vast scope for us to participate in God's metanarrative, and yet our human limitations, how do we go about making decisions about life and priorities?

---

46 Similar to the image in Zechariah 8:23 of God's people leading others from the nations into relationship with him.

Time management or …?

In a book on busyness, you'd probably expect at least one tip on time management. So here's my big tip: **don't waste your time trying to manage time**. There'll be 24 hours in a day no matter what you do.

What you *can* manage is *what you do with* the time and energy God gives you.[47] You can decide what to be busy with. As one Christian blogger puts it:

> If we want to be faithful, we have to embrace our limits as finite creatures. When the juggler has too many balls in the air, some of them have to fall. It's better to decide for yourself which balls to drop, instead of waiting for the inevitable.[48]

And because of the nature of God's metanarrative and his plan for the new creation, Point B, the most important aspect of your life for you to manage is your relationships: your relationship with God, and your relationships with the people he has placed in your life. People you can influence.

Perhaps you didn't realise you were an 'influencer'. But you are, even if you've never taken a photo of yourself posing in activewear in front of a mirror and posted it on social media. If you are a Christian, I hereby declare you a 'Point B Influencer'.

---

47 For more detail about managing your energy, see Craig Hamilton's very helpful chapter 'Time management won't help you' (chapter 16) in *Wisdom in Leadership: The how and why of leading the people you serve*.

48 R Rose, 'The overcommitment cycle', *Redeeming Productivity*, 9 September 2021, accessed 9 February 2022 (redeemingproductivity.com/the-overcommitment-cycle).

The Bible says your influence has a goal: the goal of glorifying God by helping people get to Point B, the kingdom, the new creation—transferred and transformed. And the key way in which you do that is by persistently praying for those people and teaching and modelling the biblically faithful Christian life to them. Whether it's your spouse, your kids, work colleagues, old friends, new friends, people at church, or sponsor children; whether they are Christians or non-Christians ... the good news of Jesus removing the roadblock to an eternal relationship with God, and the treasure of living in his kingdom, is for everyone.

So since you know you are an influencer, the next important step is to work out *who* you want to influence and *how*.

In a life that easily and naturally fills up with non-well-directed busyness, it's hard to be a Point B Influencer without carving out time and being—to some extent at least—intentional about it.

So I want to encourage you to do an audit.

The relationship audit

That sounds boring and annoying, doesn't it? Especially if you've ever worked in a business where the auditors come in to do their audit once a year. Nobody looks forward to that, with the possible exception of the auditors, who by and large seem to just love that sort of stuff.

"So you're telling me I've read through all those big ideas in chapters 1 to 8, and the way the rubber finally hits the road now is through an audit?! Are you kidding me?! If I'd known ..."

No, wait. Trust me, this type of audit is much more enjoyable, because it's predominantly about people whom you care for deeply.

The detail of the audit exercise is set out in the reflection section below, but the quick summary is that it's all about listing the key relationships in your life, answering some questions about each of them, and taking action to be more intentional in pursuing the Point B goal with those people.

The aim of the exercise, of course, is to highlight relationships you want to invest in, and give you a clear framework for making decisions about what you choose to be busy with each week—a framework that aligns with God's metanarrative.

Those highlighted relationships might exist in what feel like quite distinct 'arenas' of your life: family, work, sport, church, etc. But the goal is the same regardless of the arena; it's just that different arenas have different opportunities and challenges for you as a Point B Influencer. (I'll have more to say about this in the three appendices at the end of the book.)

Of course, I should mention that your audit exercise won't necessarily mean you get *busier*. The audit is not some perverse prescription for Point B workaholism. It might actually mean you decide to cut back on the number of people you are trying to spend time with, or reduce the things you are trying to get done. The audit is simply a tool to help you wisely make those sorts of assessments in the light of God's metanarrative and the part you play in it.

This is arguably the most important moment of the book—certainly in terms of applying the principles. So I urge you not to skip over this exercise, even if your intent is to come back to it later.

You know what happens in busy lives: we put important things off and it can be ages before we get to them, because life (the Evil One?) will keep throwing up one thing after another to distract us from the important.

So get out your green pen, and get busy with your audit.[49]

Reflection

Time and relationships audit exercise

A. Start by praying. Ask God to guide you as you do this exercise. Ask him to help you bring to mind the people he would have you influence and to think wisely, creatively and thoughtfully about how to do that. Pray that he will help you to be realistic in what you can do (which might mean reducing your expectations of yourself, or it might mean increasing them).

B. Next, list out the key relationships in your life in order of priority and importance. So hopefully you start at the top with God.[50] If you're married, next might be your spouse, and maybe each of your children. (Please *don't* prioritize your kids in terms of importance! Just list them

---

49 Do auditors still use green pens? If you're an auditor, and I've got this wrong and you don't use green pens any more … please don't tell me. It's a stereotype I enjoy and would like to hold on to. Thanks.

50 How is your God rest going, by the way? See chapter 3.

oldest to youngest.) Then other family members and key friends. Maybe also key work colleagues and other people you interact with quite a lot each week. Perhaps there are one or two people at church you might put on the list.

The first time you do this exercise, keep it manageable and just list a maximum of 12-15 people. If even that is too daunting, start with 3-5 people. You can always expand it later if you find you have scope to do that. Anyway, it's not actually going to be about the number of people on your list; it's going to be a function of the amount of time you need to invest in people and your own personal capacity.

If, for example, you have a child with a significant disability, your time commitment to that one person on your list might be high, and this will naturally reduce the number of other people who can be on your list.

But personal capacity also plays a part. There are people who just seem to have an enormous capacity for getting things done. We look at all they do in amazement. God just wires some people that way. (Although if pride starts driving that ultra-productivity, it can lead to significant damage.)

If you are in, or lead, a home group, put the group down as if it were one person. But if there are one or two people in your home group that you want to specifically list, do that too.

At the bottom of the list, put 'Screen time' (social media, TV/streaming, gaming, etc.) or other personal sports or hobbies that are significant consumers of your time.

My relationship with ...	Current avg time spent and what we generally do	Where is this person at with God?	Actions I could take to help them progress with God	Time I would like to spend in the future
God				
Spouse				
Child 1				
etc.				
Screen time		—	—	
Sports/ hobbies		—	—	

Next to each person, you're going to answer the questions shown above in the table headings:

- Indicate roughly how much quality time each week you spend interacting with this person/activity, and what you tend to do in that time.

- Where is this person at in their journey with God? For example: I'm actually not sure where they stand and I need to find out; definitely not a Christian; not a Christian but interested; young Christian with lots of maturing to do; steady Christian; mature Christian actively serving others in faith; Christian going through some tough things.

- Note down any ways you think you could teach or encourage them in light of where you think they are at. If you don't know where someone like a work colleague is at, you could start by asking them about their family background and whether religion played much part in it—and so hopefully find out if they have any sort of faith now. For your kids, it might be buying a good kids' Bible to read to them each evening after dinner or at bedtime. For a Christian work colleague, it might be to ask them if they'd be interested in reading the Bible with you and praying one lunchtime a week. For a family member, perhaps the step is to offer them a book that explains the Christian faith. For a neighbour or parent at school, it might be to mention your involvement at church and to invite them along some time.

- Indicate roughly how much quality time each week you would like to spend with this person in the future, and what specifically you would like to do in that time. (For some people it won't be time per week, it will be a smaller commitment, like time per month or even per year.) This is where you need to be realistic: you can't double your quality time with everyone without making some cuts. (That's why I asked you to list screens as one of your relationships. For many of us, TV/streaming/social media/gaming are areas where we fritter away quite a few hours each week. Of course, some of this may be good for relaxation; but there are other ways of relaxing that can be more effective and create more of an opportunity to build relationships—like walking, team sports, or board games.)[51]

51 Just so you know, I mention board games because I understand some people like them and think they are good for building relationships. Me, I hate them. If we ever meet, please don't ask me to play board games with you—especially those mind-bendingly complicated ones where it takes longer for me to understand the rules than it does to play the game.

- Another way to save time in your week is to invite people to come with you as you do other things. Thinking of going to a football game? Invite one of the people with whom you want to spend more time to come along, and aim to have a meaningful conversation on the way there and home in the car.
- Remember the people on your list are *people, not projects*. You may want to achieve certain things in the time you spend with them, but they may not be quite as on board with your goals. In our desire to move people towards Point B we sometimes need to 'play the long game', taking time to build the relationship and progressing slowly.

C. Once you've completed the table, review the list of action steps you might take (including praying for all these people). If it seems like too much, go back over your list and be more realistic. But once you have a list you think you can work with, make a start. Don't bite off too much too early. Begin with one or two small action steps, then gradually move on to others over time. Married couples should compare notes, and come up with a combined plan.

D. One implementation step I strongly recommend is to make an individual, personal and concrete commitment (in writing) to serve each person on your list. This will be something between you and God, not between you and the person. (You may choose to share it with the person if that seems appropriate. But do think about how it will come across to them.)

So the basic template for this written commitment is something like this:

> Because I have the joy of knowing Jesus, and I am heading to Point B, and I want [name] to get there too, I will pray [daily/weekly] for him/her, and I will encourage him/her to grow in _____
> by_____
> at least [frequency].

Here are a few examples:

- Because I have the joy of knowing Jesus, and I am heading to Point B, and I want Bob to get there too, I will pray every week for him, and I will encourage him to grow in his confidence to share his faith at work by reading a chapter of the book *40 Rockets* each week and talking about it with him by phone.

- Because I have the joy of knowing Jesus, and I am heading to Point B, and I want my son Jesse to get there too, I will pray every day for him, and I will encourage him to grow in his understanding of the gospel by reading through Romans with him three nights a week.

- Because I have the joy of knowing Jesus, and I am heading to Point B, and I want Edith to get there too, I will pray every second day for her, and I will encourage her to keep trusting the Lord in this tough time of grief she is going through by texting her an encouraging Bible verse each day.

E. Keep prayerfully reviewing your plan and commitments every two months or so, not just for progress, but for new relationships that you might want to add to your list. It might be rare that you take people off your list, but you may consciously reduce your time commitment to some people (perhaps because their need for help reduces) in order to make room for others.

Chapter by chapter summary	
1	God is our Creator and we are made in his image. We are like him, but also different.
2	God works; he is busy. God gives us, his image-bearers, work to do. Work or busyness is a good thing if it is well-directed.
3	God doesn't just work; he rests. God wants us, as his image-bearers, to rest too. Rest recognizes there is more to life than work and grants us time to enjoy God and all he gives us.
4	God has a plan, or a metanarrative, which shapes our own plan or narrative. His plan is revealed in the Bible and goes from Point A (creation) to Point B (new creation/God's kingdom).
5	Our sin stops us from getting to Point B (God's kingdom), but Jesus has transferred us there already through his death and resurrection: guaranteed. Our worth is found not in our work or activity, but in Christ's.
6	We now wait for the fulfilment of Point B—which could happen any day—being transformed day-by-day, ready for the future home of righteousness.
7	God is patiently waiting for more people to repent and be ready for the day of Point B. So we hasten that day by "abounding in the work of the Lord"—helping people to be transferred and then transformed as they wait.

8	We wait together—as the church—encouraging each other and testifying to our world together. In God's meta-narrative, the church is crucial; so it will also be top priority in our well-directed lives.
9	Decision-making about our busyness needs to be done in light of God's metanarrative and what it means for us and the people he has placed in our lives. We need to be intentional in that decision-making, or much of our busyness will be in vain.
10	
11	

10.
You're probably still thinking about it all wrong

My ambitious goal for this book so far has been to outline God's big metanarrative for the world and make the case that our lives are best lived in a way that aligns with that metanarrative. And in the previous chapter, we worked on a detailed plan for how to go about that.

Now it's possible to read those first nine chapters and think something along the following lines:

> I've got an agenda for my life that sets out my priorities, and what this book is saying is that I need to push God and ministry to others higher up my agenda. Like many preachers I've heard over the years, the author is basically calling on me to switch from something like Agenda A to something more like Agenda B.

My life agenda	My new life agenda
• family • work • house renovations • cycling/gym • church on Sundays	• God • family • church on Sundays • work • other church stuff • house renovations • cycling/gym
A	B

And that may seem like a big ask. You may even think it's a bit idealistic. Dare I suggest it is even starting to sound like the sort of radical, religious zealotry that is very unpopular in our world?

A more radical agenda

But I want to tell you that the Christianity of the Bible is even more radical than this. How is that possible?

In 2 Corinthians 5:13-15 the apostle Paul reflects on the accusation that he is making absolutely crazy (i.e. radical) life decisions. This is what he says:

> For if we are beside ourselves, it is for God; if we are in our right mind, it is for you. For the love of Christ controls us, because we have concluded this: …

So what is he going to say? What has he been so convinced of that it compels him to live a life so radical that people think he is out of his mind? We read on …

> … that one has died for all …

Of course! As you might expect, there in his motivation is the Christian gospel in a nutshell: Jesus died for us. It's John 3:16, isn't it? "God so loved the world, that he gave his only Son." And that love of Christ in dying for us is indeed very compelling.

But that's not all he's saying. There's more to it:

... that one has died for all, therefore all have ...

All have what? How would you finish that statement? Because Jesus died for all of us, therefore all of us ...? Can be forgiven? Don't have to be punished? Don't have to die? Are adopted as children of God?

Those are the sorts of (perfectly true) answers we'd give as Christians, aren't they? Because we're familiar with the idea of Jesus as our substitute—that he died in our place. And it is a wonderful and remarkable truth. But it is not the key point Paul is making here in 2 Corinthians 5. Let's read on:

... that one has died for all, therefore all have died; ...

In other words, because Jesus died, we died.

This is the idea that Jesus is not just our *substitute*; he is also our *representative*. Therefore what happens to Jesus also happens to us. Since we are united with Christ as our representative, when *he* died, *we* died. And because we are united with Christ, when *he* is resurrected to new life, *we* are resurrected to new life.

That is, in fact, what it means to be a Christian: to be united by faith with Jesus in both his death and his resurrection (Rom 6:5).

But what are the implications for us in our daily lives? Paul tells us in the next verse of 2 Corinthians 5:

> ... and he died for all, that those who live might no longer live for themselves but for him who for their sake died and was raised. (2 Cor 5:15)

This is not an isolated teaching of the apostle Paul. You see it in his letter to the Galatians as well:

> I have been crucified with Christ. It is no longer I who live, but Christ who lives in me. And the life I now live in the flesh I live by faith in the Son of God, who loved me and gave himself for me. (Gal 2:20)

The same idea of being crucified with Christ is in Romans 6:

> Do you not know that all of us who have been baptized into Christ Jesus were baptized into his death? We were buried therefore with him by baptism into death, in order that, just as Christ was raised from the dead by the glory of the Father, we too might walk in newness of life. For if we have been united with him in a death like his, we shall certainly be united with him in a resurrection like his. (Rom 6:3-5)

And these words from Romans 6 provide the background to this statement of Paul's in chapter 7:

> Likewise, my brothers, you also have died to the law through the body of Christ, so that you may belong to another, to him who has been raised from the dead, in order that we may bear fruit for God. (Rom 7:4)

If you need more convincing, see also Colossians 2:20 and 2 Timothy 2:11.

In other words, living as a Christian is not simply about moving the 'God activities' higher up the list on my agenda for my life. As I said, it's far more radical than that.

It involves the recognition that I died when Jesus died. So *my* life ended. And there's no need for an agenda for someone whose life has ended!

Having said that, we have also been *raised* in Christ. We're not lying dormant in the ground. And God does graciously give us the capacity to make decisions and set an agenda.[52]

But the mistake we are tempted to make is in thinking about it as *my* agenda for *my* life. That is a wrong way to think about it as Christians, because "it is no longer I who live, but Christ who lives in me". The life agenda we adopt has to now be thought of as **Jesus' agenda for his life in me**.

As Christians, we must relinquish any sense of entitlement to the control of our lives or the setting of our own priorities, whilst at the same time thoughtfully setting priorities and making choices about what we do.

It's a radically different way of thinking about life—one that is massively countercultural and splendidly liberating (Rom 6:6-7).[53] From childhood our culture teaches us that

---

52 This is fortunate, because the last nine chapters would have been pointless if that weren't the case.

53 Superficially, of course, it may look the same. It might still involve moving God and church up the agenda in priority (as per Agenda B earlier). But the underlying way of thinking is fundamentally different and that will show itself in important ways.

we are masters of our own destiny, and that we ought to pursue our own dreams, follow our own heart, and strive to be anything we want to be in order to find happiness.

Such mindsets are not just unrealistic, they are enslaving, playing as they do on our sin and selfishness. They are a million miles away from living no longer for myself, but for him who died for me and was raised (2 Cor 5:15).

This Christian mindset is so countercultural, the reality of it is hard for us to genuinely grasp. So I encourage you to go back and read the last few pages again and ponder them deeply. Look up the Bible passages in their context, and check what God is saying. Because if this is true, it's a profoundly different way of approaching life.

Thinking right

What I have tried to do in this book is not so much give you practical tips on how not to be a workaholic, or advice about getting more sleep, or for reducing the frenetic pace of family life. There are lots of books that offer good, helpful advice on those sorts of areas.[54]

Rather, what I've tried to do is give you a biblical framework for how you think about life—a framework that provides a basis for making day-to-day decisions about what you will be busy with. I've tried to get you thinking about what the Bible says about God's agenda and your part in it.

And this chapter presents what I think is possibly the most fundamental, challenging, practical and frequently

54 I have, however, tried to give a few further practical thoughts in chapter 11 and in the appendices.

missed truth that you need to come to terms with as a follower of Jesus: **it is no longer you who live, but Christ who lives in you.**

So do you still think of your life as your own to make choices about? Do you still think it's up to you what you're busy with?

Because if you do, some of your Christian thinking is still immature and underdeveloped, and hopefully God will change that.

"Whoa! Who are you to say something like that?!" might be your understandable reaction.

Well, it's not actually me saying it. This is the point of Paul's words in Philippians:

> Let those of us who are mature think this way, and if in anything you think otherwise, God will reveal that also to you. Only let us hold true to what we have attained. (Phil 3:15-16)

What is "this way" of thinking which Paul says reflects a high level of maturity as Christians? What is the mindset that he longs for them all to have?

There are two really helpful clues as to what Paul means.[55]

As you'd expect, the first clue is in the immediately

---

55 I am indebted to John Piper for his very helpful explanation of Philippians 3:15-16 in the following two talks:
- 'What does it mean to be mature? Philippians 3:15-16', *Desiring God*, 22 June 2019 (youtube.com/watch?v=a3L1Qi1d6VI)
- 'What the mature think about: Philippians 3:15-16', *Desiring God*, 25 June 2019 (youtube.com/watch?v=Run7kN8tIeE).

preceding verses, in which he talks about his goals. Paul's personal desire is that he "may know him [i.e. Christ] and the power of his resurrection" (v 10). Everything else that he previously thought gave his life meaning—what he was busy with—these days he considers "rubbish" (v 8).[56] What's important to him now is knowing Christ: the Lord who humbled himself and went to the cross for our sake and rose again to give us a new life (2:6-11).

Then he says his other priority is to share in Christ's "sufferings, becoming like him in his death" (v 10). That's not an expression of rampant masochism by Paul. It's not that he *wants* to suffer and die. It's his way of talking about his life—a life of sacrificing himself for the sake of ministry to others. It's the life he talked about back in Philippians 1:25, which is lived at great personal cost for the "progress and joy in the faith" of other people.

The second clue is that the same word behind "think this way" (or "have this mind/mindset") is also used twice back in Philippians 2: "being in full accord and of one **mind**" (v 2) and "Have this **mind** among yourselves" (v 5).[57] And what is the mindset he is calling on them to have back in chapter 2? It's the mindset of the Lord Jesus himself, who "humbled himself by becoming obedient to the point of death, even death on a cross" (v 8).

What Paul is saying is this: although he has not perfected that servant mindset in himself (3:12-13), he 'presses on', knowing that ultimately it leads to the "prize

---

56 That's the polite English word! You could also translate it as 'dung'.

57 Greek: φρονέω (*phroneō*). This Greek word also appears in Philippians 3:19 and 4:2.

of the upward call of God in Christ Jesus" (v 14). And he wants you to have the same mindset.

In so doing, we are simply following the mindset and example of our Lord Jesus, and "becoming like him in his death"—humbly sacrificing our lives for the sake of others.

If you don't yet fully have that mindset, may God reveal it to you soon, as you continue to live true to the Christian understanding that you "have attained" to this point. Keep pressing on in developing that mature Christian mindset.

That's not me saying it. It's God.

Reflection

1. If you are a Christian, did you know you had already died? How do you feel about this?

2. In what areas do you think you are still living for yourself instead of for him who died for you?

3. If your choices about what to be busy with each day were based on Jesus' agenda for his life in you instead of your agenda, how would they be different?

4. How hard do you find it to have a mindset like Jesus and Paul? What could help with this?

5. How do you think your family and friends will react if you start living life with that radical mindset? How do you think the Bible suggests they will react? See for example:

- Matthew 10:16-25
- Luke 6:22-23
- John 17:14
- John 20:18-21
- 2 Timothy 3:12

6. How should you react to their reaction? See:
   - 1 Peter 3:13-17, 4:12-19
   - Matthew 5:44
   - Romans 12:14-21
   - Revelation 2:9-11

7. Confess to God your past and present reluctance to give up your life, and ask him for his help in making changes.

Chapter by chapter summary	
1	God is our Creator and we are made in his image. We are like him, but also different.
2	God works; he is busy. God gives us, his image-bearers, work to do. Work or busyness is a good thing if it is well-directed.
3	God doesn't just work; he rests. God wants us, as his image-bearers, to rest too. Rest recognizes there is more to life than work and grants us time to enjoy God and all he gives us.
4	God has a plan, or a metanarrative, which shapes our own plan or narrative. His plan is revealed in the Bible and goes from Point A (creation) to Point B (new creation/God's kingdom).

5	Our sin stops us from getting to Point B (God's kingdom), but Jesus has transferred us there already through his death and resurrection: guaranteed. Our worth is found not in our work or activity, but in Christ's.
6	We now wait for the fulfilment of Point B—which could happen any day—being transformed day-by-day, ready for the future home of righteousness.
7	God is patiently waiting for more people to repent and be ready for the day of Point B. So we hasten that day by "abounding in the work of the Lord"—helping people to be transferred and then transformed as they wait.
8	We wait together—as the church—encouraging each other and testifying to our world together. In God's meta-narrative, the church is crucial; so it will also be top priority in our well-directed lives.
9	Decision-making about our busyness needs to be done in light of God's metanarrative and what it means for us and the people he has placed in our lives. We need to be intentional in that decision-making, or much of our busyness will be in vain.
10	The Christian perspective on what we do with our time and resources is far more radical (and liberating) than we often think. It recognizes that in Christ our lives have ended; so our agenda is that of Christ, who lives in us.
11	

11.
"Yes, but ..."

All the way back in the introduction, I asked why you picked up this book. What were the pressure points that made you think, "Yeah, I think I might read that"?

And back in that introduction, I explained what I was setting out to do:

> I want to avoid magic bullets and instead look with you at what God has to say in the Bible about busyness.

But I wonder, as we're now on the home stretch and heading towards the end of the book, what you are feeling and whether you've found the help you were hoping for.

"Sure," I hear you say, "I appreciate the biblical principles, and I didn't expect magic bullets, but I was hoping you could give me something a little more concrete to help me. You just seem to be saying do more well-directed Christian activity! All this theology is good and fine, but how do I solve my busyness problem? Come on, can't you see I'm really struggling here?"

More?

Firstly, no, no, no! Please understand I'm *not* saying, "Do more Christian activities".

Whether you're going to be *more* busy or *less* busy as a result of this book is a matter for *you* to assess, not me.

I actually hope that many of you *reduce* your level of activity—a little more Mary and a little less Martha[58] would be a pretty common prescription, I suspect. Plus a little more God rest.

But much more importantly, I hope that whatever level of busyness you decide to adopt, it is *well-directed* busyness.

Indeed, the goal of the major audit exercise at the end of chapter 9 is to help you assess what's realistic and achievable. That might well mean cuts rather than additions. And the whole point of outlining a Christian perspective (i.e. on how we fit into God's metanarrative) is to help you assess what opportunities are on offer and make wise choices between them, knowing you can't possibly do them all.

Furthermore, the call to gospel urgency (particularly in chapter 7) must not be read in isolation from what we learned in the opening chapters about rest. Remember my pastor friend's catch-cry: "There's only one saviour of the world, and it's not you!" That's an important perspective to maintain.

For some of us, God gave us a seemingly infinite capacity to see the needs around us and a very limited capacity to say 'no'. But God also made us with a finite capacity to

58 See chapter 3.

meet those needs, and we need to recognize that the sovereign, omnipotent God of the universe can manage to get things done without us if necessary!

Others of us are so oblivious to the needs around us we don't even realize we're being asked to do something when someone says, "Can you please ...?" If that's your issue, you need to recognize there is a war going on, and step into the battle with more intent.

All that said, if you are really struggling under a heavy weight of busyness at the moment, close to burning out, let me offer a few further practical thoughts.

Busy with the everyday stuff of life

A pretty common reaction to chapters 1 to 10, particularly among people in certain seasons of life, might be something like this:

> I see what you're saying, and I do want to fill my life with Point B busyness, but when I look at my daily routine, so much of it is filled with the everyday stuff of life: cooking, cleaning, laundry, caring for a sick family member, paying bills, raking leaves, etcetera, etcetera. And once I deal with all that inevitable stuff, on many days there just doesn't seem there's much time left for the disciple-making activities you're urging me to do.

What can we say about that type of very understandable reaction?

Fallen life is complex life

The first thing I want to admit is that life is much more complex than the nice, neat, straight-line metanarrative outlined in this book might lead us to imagine.

We live in a fallen world, a world in which—as we saw in chapter 2—there is significant frustration, including with what we perceive to be our best-conceived and most God-aligned plans. Even with the highest degree of intentionality, we simply can't achieve all that we would like to achieve.

> Many are the plans in the mind of a man,
> > but it is the purpose of the Lord that will stand.
> (Prov 19:21)

So, for example, you intend to meet with a non-Christian friend to read the Bible and help him transfer to Point B. But at the last minute your toddler falls sick, and you need to take her to the doctor, go and buy the medicine, and then battle to get her to swallow that medicine every few hours when she stubbornly refuses. Next comes the paperwork to make a claim on your health insurance—the insurance you prudently spent hours researching because you know you live in a fallen world where sickness inevitably comes along. But the insurance company messes it up, and you spend two hours on the phone trying to sort it out.

Sound familiar? We've all experienced this sort of reality. The fallen state of the world is a black hole—it sucks our time into it and our time isn't ever coming back out of that sucker. It's gone.

It's a fallen world, and that just makes life harder. This reality shouldn't take us by surprise, even if it frustrates us. After all, it was God's intention after Adam and Eve sinned.[59]

Love, laundry and the long-term view

But it doesn't even have to be something going wrong. There are lots of activities—like cooking and doing laundry —that just go hand-in-hand with our God-given responsibilities to care for our family and for others, or to serve our employer, or to be a good citizen.[60]

When you sit down with your 5-year-old son, or with your non-Christian work colleague, to open the Bible and read it with them, it's very easy to see the connection to Point B. But when you're changing your baby's fifth diaper for the morning, the connection seems ... well, let's just say you might need binoculars or even a telescope to see it from here.

This is where 1 Corinthians 13 gives us an important corrective:

> If I speak in the tongues of men and of angels, but have not love, I am a noisy gong or a clanging cymbal. And if I have prophetic powers, and understand all mysteries and all knowledge, and if I have all faith, so as to remove mountains, but have not love, I am nothing. If I give away all I have, and if I deliver

59 That's the nature of the curse God imposed in Genesis 3:17-19.
60 I have more to say about family responsibilities in appendix 3.

up my body to be burned, but have not love, I gain nothing. (1 Cor 13:1-3)

Or, if I might paraphrase using the terminology of chapter 7:

If I prayerfully persevere in proclaiming Christ to people, focusing my life on the four Ps, but have not love, I am a noisy gong or a clanging symbol.

Of course, we believe with all our heart that prayerfully proclaiming Christ to people is indeed a loving thing to do.[61] But to say to your 5-year-old, "Get your own dinner, wash your own clothes, and then we'll read the Bible and I'll help you understand God's love for you" seems a little hollow and perverse, does it not?

While my caring actions (e.g. making dinner for the family) need to be accompanied by the teachable truths that help people rightly interpret my actions, the idea that we can teach them the gospel of Christ's love and yet not live it out in day-to-day loving actions is clearly absurd (as James 2 makes clear).

---

61 "There can be no artificial distinction between 'love' as the basic shape of Christian character, and 'ministry' as the basic activity of Christian fellowship. The gospel reveals the ultimate good that is found in God and in the kingdom of his crucified and risen Son—and so we speak the truth in love to everyone around us in order to build Christ's body. We want to see everyone around us come to know Christ, and to become strong in faith, love and hope in him, because that is the great 'good' of all our lives. It's what we were all made for." T Payne, 'What love really is: And why it is the essence of Christian living', *The Payneful Truth*, 15 September 2021, accessed 9 February 2022 (thepaynefultruth. online/p/what-love-really-is).

In part, this is just the straightforward principle of needing to model what we are teaching—to not be hypocrites—showing the people around us what the grace of God looks like in meeting all sorts of needs.

Love also involves taking the long-term view—the view that requires that fourth P, perseverance.

So when changing the baby's fifth diaper you might indeed require a telescope to see how it helps anyone get to Point B. But, if that's the case, then get out God's telescope and take a look through it.

Seeing things through that telescope is to 'live by faith' (Hab 2:4)—to use a biblical phrase. It is accepting that we don't know, and certainly can't predict, all the twists and turns of God's metanarrative as God applies it to an individual's life. But we trust God's sovereignty and his assurance that when we fulfil the responsibilities he gives us, he uses that—sometimes mysteriously and surprisingly—to bring about his metanarrative end point. Sometimes that God-given responsibility involves reading the Bible with someone; sometimes it involves changing a diaper.

Having said that, it's important to affirm three important points.

Firstly, it is the message of the gospel that is the power to save and transfer people (Rom 1:16) into God's kingdom. So teaching people that message and praying for them to respond with faith must remain a priority within all the circumstances and responsibilities God places us in. Jesus demonstrated this when he chose to prioritize preaching even over meeting people's need for healing (Mark 1:32-39). That we may not be able to do as much direct gospel influencing as we would hope does not mean we should give up prioritizing it.[62]

Secondly, there is a lot we can do—even while attending to all that stuff of life—that is more obviously connected to Point B influencing. Praying for your baby as you change all those diapers not only helps you feel less frustrated, not only reminds you to take a long-term view of the life of your child, but—because prayer "has great power as it is working" (Jas 5:16)—it actively partners with God in bringing about his plans and purposes for your child. You could make a pastoral phone call while you do laundry. Or prepare for your Bible study group during your commute to work. A bit of creative multitasking like this can even reduce some of the tedium of those life tasks.

I wonder if this is the sort of attitude (even if not the specific examples) the apostle Paul had in mind when he talked about "making the best use of the time" in Ephesians 5:16 and Colossians 4:5? He literally says "redeem the time" or "rescue the time from being lost", especially through speaking 'salty' words (Col 4:6)—that is, words of Point B influence.

Thirdly, there is more you can change than you think. That is, not everything you think is the unavoidable stuff of life necessarily belongs in that category.[63] I'll say more about this below.

---

62 I say 'direct' gospel influencing because of course our loving actions towards people can, under God, be an indirect gospel influence. It's the Titus 2:10 idea of making the teaching about God our saviour attractive (as the NIV puts it).

63 Just to be clear, changing the baby's diaper actually *is* in that category.

Ask for help

For a significant percentage of readers, your busyness problem might be at the point where it has become a serious issue. It could, for example, be causing or contributing to mental health struggles, particularly burnout, anxiety and depression.[64] Or it might be causing other stress-related health problems.

If that's where you're at right now, the first thing to do is ask for help.

Start by asking for God's help. Pray about it.

If there are health issues, one of the people to seek help from is your personal physician. Getting on top of those physical or mental health concerns is crucial. Other steps will be very hard to make progress on without first dealing with those health challenges.

Once you are dealing with any health issues, think of the wisest Christian person you know who might be accessible to you, and ask if you could talk to them.[65] Openly share your struggle with them and ask them to help you think things through and pray with and for you.

Maybe you could read this book with them, and talk and pray about it together? Maybe they could help you with your audit exercise? That exercise is really key, but it can also be daunting to undertake on your own if you are

---

64 If anxiety is an issue for you, I would particularly like to recommend that you read Paul Grimmond's book *When the Noise Won't Stop: A Christian guide to dealing with anxiety.*

65 The worst that could happen is they say no. And if they do, at least you've had a valuable lesson in how to say no! Just move on to the next wisest person.

already feeling under pressure.

Maybe just the act of sharing with someone and having them pray with you and for you will be a sufficient turning point in relieving some pressure.

And, hey, listen up: don't go getting all super-spiritual on me at this point. None of this "Oh, I'll just depend on God and trust him to be my help. I won't spill my guts to anyone and burden them." The most common way God helps us is through his faithful and caring people. It's not either/or. You can, and almost certainly *should*, do both.

Look for the driver

Calm down, golfers. Not *that* sort of driver. I'm not suggesting you down tools and go and play some golf. (Although, now that I think about it ...)

What I mean is, look for the underlying issues that are driving you to the problematic level of busyness you have found yourself in.

Let me give you an example. Some years ago I was working crazy hours, and really starting to unravel in terms of stress and health. What was the driver? Answer: I was passionately committed to the work I was doing at Matthias Media, and desperately wanted it to succeed. No doubt my self-esteem was also unhealthily caught up in that desire for the ministry to succeed. So the more our financial struggles grew, the harder and harder I worked to try to get us out of it.

But I didn't do what I just told you to do; I didn't ask for help.

Until one day I found myself in tears in my father's

office and sharing with him the stress I and the company were under.

I didn't need to ask him for help at that point; he was onto it straightaway. We identified some of the main problems, and found and implemented solutions. But I *did* need to *tell someone* in order to get that help, and I still remember him gently reminding me that day about the importance of asking for help when things start to get on top of you. Lesson learned. (Mostly.)

But the driver that pushed me to that emotional breaking point was not my busyness as such, or commitment to the business for that matter. The driver was my desire to succeed, or perhaps more accurately, to *not fail* and let certain people down—people whom I really wanted to think well of me. Self-esteem was very much part of my busyness equation. My personal sense of worth was all tangled up in my work.

Sometimes the driver is something as simple as financial pressure, even without any self-esteem issues magnifying it. The need to work multiple jobs just to pay the bills certainly has the potential to make you feel unhealthily busy. Maybe a financial planner is the person you need to talk to?

Or the driver might be a real love for your kids, and desperately wanting them to have a better life than you did, full of meaningful and valuable experiences.[66] That certainly also has the potential to make you feel unhealthily busy.

Or the driver might be an addiction. Is there, for

66 I also make some suggestions about this in appendix 3.

example, an addiction to pornography or gaming or social media that is not just sinful and unhealthy, but actually eating up many hours of your life and adding to your sense of busyness?

Of course, looking for, and finding, the driver of your busyness doesn't always solve the problem. Financial pressures don't disappear just because you identify them as a cause. Nor do self-esteem issues tend to resolve quickly.

But recognizing and naming the drivers is still helpful. It gives you the chance to at least better understand why you are feeling pushed in the directions you are. It also gives you the chance to bring those issues out of the darkness where they are hiding away, and beneficially subject them to some critical scrutiny, again perhaps with the help of a wise Christian friend.

You'll also want to scrutinize your drivers under the sharp light of God's word. Perhaps they are symptoms of an underlying anxiety that needs to be brought to God in prayer (Phil 4:6-7)? Or perhaps they come from a sinful and idolatrous attitude that needs to be repented of.

So when your busyness feels like a heavy burden, ask a simple diagnostic question: Why am I doing all this?

More can change than you think

The last point I'd make is that it is very easy to feel you are trapped; to feel that there really are very few choices you can make that will alleviate your busyness. Most of us—of a certain age—are familiar with that feeling of being the hamster on the treadmill, and feeling like there's no way off it.

I want to suggest to you that this sense of being trapped

is frequently misguided. There is *almost always* a solution. It's just that the solution comes with a cost we are not prepared to pay.

Sometimes it is the perceived cost more than the actual cost. By way of example, I remember my first job after university. It was a reasonably well-paid professional job, with good prospects for progression to partnership in the firm. But towards the end of that first year in the job, I had a phone call. Would I consider leaving my job to work as an administrator for a church (that happened to be starting a publishing ministry)? Less pay. Only a two-year contract.

It felt at the time like such a major and costly career decision.

It wasn't.

In hindsight, it was never a career-ending choice, and the job I left behind really was an unsatisfying rat-race that I wasn't enjoying in the slightest.

The perceived cost of the change was high. But in reality it wasn't really such a big deal. And God provided in ways I could never have anticipated.[67]

Or think, for example, of the family with the onerous mortgage payments. The financial pressure drives both parents to work full-time. That inevitably imposes a sense of stressful busyness which pervades their household.

The mortgage commitment is very often driven by a

---

67 By the way, it's worth noting that the job I left was a busy one. And the new job I started at the church was a busy one. My busyness didn't really change. But the new job undoubtedly aligned better with God's metanarrative.

longing to give children a happy place to grow up, each child with their own room, a nice backyard in which to play, and close to a good school.

Not that there's anything inherently wrong with that longing. (Authors in glass houses ... as they say.)

But that stressful busyness could be alleviated by downsizing and moving to a less expensive home, allowing one parent to perhaps drop down to part-time work. And, you know what, it might just be good for the kids to be in the same bedroom. In fact, the vast majority of kids in the world are content, even happy, doing that. If you asked most kids, they'd tell you they would much prefer extra time with Mum and Dad, even if it means living in a more modest home.

But how many Christian families do you know who make that choice—whether to alleviate their busyness or to make more time for ministry endeavours?

Not many? Any?

And why? We don't want to pay the (perceived) cost.

Have we forgotten the treasure that lies buried in our future?

So all that said ...

I do still want to push you back to the main goal of this book—thinking critically about your choices and doing so from the perspective God has given us in his word. God has graciously "[made] known to us the mystery of his will, according to his purpose, which he set forth in Christ as a plan for the fullness of time, to unite all things in him, things in heaven and things on earth" (Eph 1:9-10). So why would we not use that wise insight and perspective to make good decisions about what we do with our time today? And tomorrow. And the next day.

In his letter to the church in Laodicea, Jesus speaks these chilling words:

> "You are neither cold nor hot. Would that you were either cold or hot. So, because you are luke-warm, and neither hot nor cold, I will spit [literally "vomit"] you out of my mouth." (Rev 3:15-16)

But what is it that has caused Jesus to come to that scathing assessment of them? Has he taken the temperature of their hearts and found that their passion or love towards him has waned? Is it about their emotions?

I omitted the first four words of verse 15, which give us the answer: "I know your *works* …", he says. Jesus sees what they *do*, their activities, what they are *busy* with—and that's what he is challenging them about. If only they had some ointment for their eyes so they might more clearly see the spiritual realities of their lives (Rev 3:18), then they might hear Jesus' voice and "be zealous and repent" (Rev 3:19; see also Titus 2:11-14).

It's so easy to be busy with, and even zealous about, the *wrong things*.

Instead, let's get our zeal and busyness well-directed towards Point B, and heed the apostle Paul's instruction and example: "Do not be slothful in zeal, be fervent in spirit, serve the Lord" (Rom 12:11).

The restful yoke

As we finish, I want to return to some important words of Jesus that we looked at briefly back in chapter 5. Jesus makes an invitation:

> "Come to me, all who labour and are heavy laden, and I will give you rest." (Matt 11:28)

To those of you who feel the heavy burden of busyness in this fallen and frustrating world, who feel the burden and frustration of your own personal fallenness, who feel the burden of law keeping, Jesus promises you *rest*.

If you were an ox, and you pulled the plough all day, you would probably picture rest as having the yoke lifted off your tired and aching shoulders, heading to your nice, comfortable stall, and putting your hooves up.[68] No more work for you.

But that's not what Jesus says:

> "Take my yoke upon you, and learn from me, for I am gentle and lowly in heart, and you will find rest for your souls. For my yoke is easy, and my burden is light." (Matt 11:29-30)

There's still a yoke. The work is not all done. The rest is for our *souls*, not our bodies.

But as we take on this new yoke, the direction of that work is set by Jesus as we "learn from" him. It is *his* yoke;

---

68 The yoke is the wooden frame that connects two animals together when they are working. The two who are yoked have to go in the same direction. That's why Paul says not to be yoked to unbelievers, as they may push or pull you in ungodly directions (2 Cor 6:14-18).

it connects us to him, so that our work is alongside Jesus; and the direction he goes in, we go in. If the direction Jesus took was to give up his life to serve and bring people to Point B, as his followers our direction becomes to give up our lives to serve and work with the risen Lord Jesus as he brings people to Point B. We tread the same path.

Since this labour is done for him and alongside him— that is, the one to whom all things have been handed over by God the Father (Matt 11:27)—this yoke is easy. His burden is light.

No longer are we doing the cursed work that is hard and heavy (Gen 3:17-19), we are doing "the work of the Lord" (1 Cor 15:58) that is fruitful into eternity because Jesus is in charge of all things.

Does that mean doing the work of the Lord and making disciples is 'easy'? No; for one thing it means being hated and persecuted (John 15:18-20; 2 Tim 3:12). Jesus' work of dying on the cross was not easy, therefore neither is the work of his followers.

But in another sense it *is* easy because we're not doing it to justify ourselves. Part of what makes our yoke so burdensome is how much can be at stake. But we're not working to prove our worth. Our worth is found in being God's adopted children for whom Christ died. My relationship with him is not dependent on my usefulness to him.

And it is also easy in the sense that we are no longer working *against* God in rebellion, but working *with* him towards the fulfilment of his metanarrative.

He *will* get it done. So our burden is light. Therefore take his yoke upon yourself and find rest for your soul.

Reflection

1. After your chapter 9 audit will you be reducing, reallocating or increasing your busyness? How do you feel about that?

2. If you were ever to feel overwhelmed by busyness, who could you ask for help?

3. Which activities in your "unavoidable stuff of life" category are really avoidable? Should you drop them?

4. How can you "redeem" more time?

5. What drives the bulk of your busyness? Is it right to be driven by those things?

6. Assessed by your activities, are you "lukewarm"? Why/why not?

Chapter by chapter summary	
1	God is our Creator and we are made in his image. We are like him, but also different.
2	God works; he is busy. God gives us, his image-bearers, work to do. Work or busyness is a good thing if it is well-directed.
3	God doesn't just work; he rests. God wants us, as his image-bearers, to rest too. Rest recognizes there is more to life than work and grants us time to enjoy God and all he gives us.

4	God has a plan, or a metanarrative, which shapes our own plan or narrative. His plan is revealed in the Bible and goes from Point A (creation) to Point B (new creation/God's kingdom).
5	Our sin stops us from getting to Point B (God's kingdom), but Jesus has transferred us there already through his death and resurrection: guaranteed. Our worth is found not in our work or activity, but in Christ's.
6	We now wait for the fulfilment of Point B—which could happen any day—being transformed day-by-day, ready for the future home of righteousness.
7	God is patiently waiting for more people to repent and be ready for the day of Point B. So we hasten that day by "abounding in the work of the Lord"—helping people to be transferred and then transformed as they wait.
8	We wait together—as the church—encouraging each other and testifying to our world together. In God's meta-narrative, the church is crucial; so it will also be top priority in our well-directed lives.
9	Decision-making about our busyness needs to be done in light of God's metanarrative and what it means for us and the people he has placed in our lives. We need to be intentional in that decision-making, or much of our busyness will be in vain.
10	The Christian perspective on what we do with our time and resources is far more radical (and liberating) than we often think. It recognizes that in Christ our lives have ended; so our agenda is that of Christ, who lives in us.
11	If you're feeling trapped in a bad place in terms of stress and busyness: think long-term, ask for help, look for the 'drivers', and accept the reality that you can probably change more than you think.

Recommended resources

Chapter 3: Made in God's image to rest

Liggins, Stephen, *The Good Sporting Life: Loving and playing sport as a follower of Jesus*, Matthias Media

Chapter 4: God's metanarrative

Goldsworthy, Graeme, *Gospel and Kingdom: A Christian interpretation of the Old Testament*, Paternoster Press

Roberts, Vaughan, *God's Big Picture: Tracing the storyline of the Bible*, IVP

Robson, Geoff, *The Book of Books: A short guide to reading the Bible*, Matthias Media

Chapter 5: The roadblock removed

Lynch, Mikey, *The Good Life in the Last Days: Making choices when the time is short*, Matthias Media

Chapter 7: How to hasten the day

Cheng, Gordon, *Encouragement: How words change lives*, Matthias Media

Marshall, Colin and Tony Payne, *The Vine Project: Shaping your ministry culture around disciple-making*, Matthias Media

Orr, Peter, 'Abounding in the work of the Lord (1 Cor 15:58): Everything we do as Christians or specific gospel work?', *Themelios*, 2013, 38(2):205-214

Orr, Peter, 'The work of the Lord', *The Briefing*, 2014, 413:19-24

Chapter 9: Intentional relationships

Hamilton, Craig, 'Time management won't help you' (chapter 16), in *Wisdom in Leadership: The how and why of leading the people you serve*, Matthias Media

Chapter 11: "Yes, but …"

Grimmond, Paul, *When the Noise Won't Stop: A Christian guide to dealing with anxiety*, Matthias Media

Appendices: busyness, paid employment, church, and family life

Robson, Geoff, *Thank God for Bedtime: What God says about our sleep and why it matters more than you think*, Matthias Media

Appendix 1: Paid employment

Grimmond, Paul, 'God's plan for work: The cultural mandate', *The Briefing*, 2013, 406:16-21

Grimmond, Paul, 'Vocation? What's that?', *The Briefing*, 2013, 407:14-20

Grimmond, Paul 'Work, value, and the gospel', *The Briefing*, 2014, 409:14-19

Josling, Craig, *40 Rockets: Encouragement and tips for turbo-charging your evangelism at work*, Matthias Media

Liggins, Stephen, *The Good Sporting Life: Loving and playing sport as a follower of Jesus*, Matthias Media

Taylor, William, *Revolutionary Work: What's the point of the 9 to 5?*, 10Publishing

Appendix 2: Church

Carswell, Roger, *And Some Evangelists: Growing your church through discovering and developing evangelists*, Christian Focus

Payne, Tony, *How to Walk into Church*, Matthias Media

Helm, David, *One-to-One Bible Reading: A simple guide for every Christian*, Matthias Media

Appendix 3: Family life

Blowes, Peter, 'The Swedish Method', *The Briefing*, 2009, 364:16-21

Carmichael, Stephanie, Books for Little Ones series, Matthias Media

Nielson, Jon, *Bible Reading with Your Kids: A simple guide for every father*, Matthias Media

Appendices:
busyness, paid employment, church, and family life

The good thing about God's metanarrative is that it is *meta*. It's the big story that overarches *every* aspect of our own personal story. There is, therefore, no aspect of our lives where it is not the applicable metanarrative.

That saves me a lot of work as the author of this book, because the principles I have outlined apply to every arena of our lives. I don't need to set out principles for people at high school, and different principles for people who work in a bank, and others for those who are single, and so on.

If the principles are clear enough, you should be able to prayerfully apply them to your own current situation using your God-given wisdom and the wise input of some of your Christian brothers and sisters.

Nonetheless, I thought it might be worth including some thoughts on some of the more common arenas of life: paid employment, church, and family life.[69]

In particular—since our audit exercise at the end of chapter 9 will have inevitably focused our attention on key work, church and family relationships—**I want to spend some time with you thinking through how to help the people you relate to in those areas to take steps towards Point B.** That's what most of these three appendices will be about.

But before we dive in, let me preface what follows with this caution: a lot of what is in these appendices is just my own personal thoughts. (Or wisdom? You be the judge.) I hope a lot of what I say *flows* from biblical principles. But I feel like I need to follow the apostle Paul's example (in 1 Cor 7:12) and point out that it is "I, not the Lord" who is saying much of this. If you think otherwise on some of this advice, this time that's perfectly okay with me.

---

69 The other arena we spend a lot of our time in is sleep. (Or maybe not.) Sleep is therefore an important matter to think through as a Christian. The best book—in fact the only book—I know that helpfully reflects on this topic biblically is *Thank God for Bedtime: What God says about our sleep and why it matters more than you think* by Geoff Robson.

Appendix 1.
Paid employment

Let me be clear from the outset that when I use the word 'work' in this appendix, unlike earlier in the book, I do not mean labour or activity of *any* sort. I am particularly thinking about regular, paid employment engaged in for a significant proportion of your week. Being a stay-at-home parent or a full-time student, for example, also involves effort or 'work', but in this appendix that is not what I am addressing.

I also am thinking of 'secular' work rather than the work of ministry, even though the latter often involves paid employment. Ministry work has some extra complexities and nuances that need special consideration. Some of what I say may have a degree of applicability to those in paid gospel work. But if that's you, please apply what I say with due regard for those complexities.

The changing work context

The first thing we need to acknowledge in thinking about work is that patterns have changed over time and they are continuing to change.

On average, people in Australia, the United Kingdom and the United States are working fewer hours than they were, say, 30 years ago.[70] Some of that decline is from people working part-time instead of full-time—not always by choice.

Even though the statistics might show a slight reduction in average hours worked, for many workers the line between work and personal time has blurred because of the 'always on' communication technology we use in our working lives these days. So for some workers it is quite hard to determine how many hours they are working each week, and it is often significantly more than the statistics might suggest.

Work-related stress is also being increasingly recognized as a major problem, particularly in some professions (e.g. the medical profession).

In 2019, the World Health Organization defined burn-out as a "syndrome conceptualized as resulting from chronic workplace stress that has not been successfully managed".[71] The common characteristics of it are:

- feelings of energy depletion or exhaustion

70 OECD, *Hours worked (indicator)* [data set], OECD website, 2022, doi: 10.1787/47be1c78-en, accessed 9 February 2022 (data.oecd.org/emp/hours-worked.htm).
71 World Health Organization, *Burn-out an "occupational phenomenon": International Classification of Diseases*, WHO website, 28 May 2019, accessed 9 February 2022 (who.int/news/item/28-05-2019-burn-out-an-occupational-phenomenon-international-classification-of-diseases). If you have some of these symptoms, it might be time to talk to someone about it (as I suggested in chapter 11).

- increased mental distance from one's job, or feelings of negativism or cynicism related to one's job
- reduced professional efficacy.

So work even gets its own syndrome these days!

But the good news is that there is also an emerging awareness of burnout and a push-back against unhealthy work stress and the encroachment of work into personal time. I read recently of one CEO who personally will gently rebuke any employee he discovers replying to work emails outside of normal work hours.

So, fortunately, work–life balance has 'become a thing' in recent years, along with better understanding of how to manage stress. Employers are recognizing that these issues matter to their staff and affect staff retention rates. More than that, many now recognize that overworking and unhappiness in their staff negatively impacts productivity.

Regrettably, not every employer is so enlightened, and so for many of us our paid employment remains a very large contributor to our sense of overwhelming busyness.

But, of course, our work experiences are very varied. And that variation means it's a little hard to give specific advice about how much work might be too much. But there are still some points worth making.

Work: how much is too much?

I remember many years ago going to hear a talk given by Steve Biddulph, an Australian psychologist and author of multiple books about parenting, including the very helpful book *Raising Boys*. Biddulph was speaking to a large audience of fathers. Admittedly he was speaking in a venue on the North Shore of Sydney, which would have skewed the audience demographic towards a middle/upper-middle-class group of professional workers. And it was in an era when working long hours was definitely a badge of honour—especially for men.[72]

Biddulph was well into his talk on fatherhood, having given lots of useful advice and tips, when he paused for dramatic effect and emphatically made a comment that went something like this: "If you work more than 45 hours per week, you won't be a good father to your children".

You know that noise an audience makes when it hears something a little troubling or controversial? I heard it then. It was the noise of hundreds of men all simultaneously sucking in air through semi-pursed lips, and realizing he was talking about them.

The point was not the exact number of hours;[73] the point was the stark statement of the expert opinion that at a certain point your work will negatively affect your chil-

---

72 At the professional firm I worked for briefly back then (in the late 1980s), if you were observed leaving around the 'official' finish time for work (about 5.30pm), the expected call from those still sitting in their cubicles was "You leaving?" (said with a very-much-intended surprised intonation). To which the expected (untrue) reply was "Just off to see a client". It was all said in jest, but the undercurrent was crystal clear. Nobody was in any doubt that the longer you worked, the more serious you were seen to be about progressing in the firm. For some reason my staff review generally involved the comment "You seem to lack ambition".

73 To be honest, I can't remember the exact wording of what he said, or the exact number of hours. But it was definitely something like this. It didn't seem like a massively high number at the time.

dren. To a bunch of guys who I'm sure genuinely wanted to be good fathers (why else would they have been in the room?), it was a shocking wake-up call.

Of course, it's not simply about 'hours worked', by which most people mean 'hours at work'. Another big factor is travel time. So the important figure, especially for parents, is not how many hours per week you work, it's how many hours per week you spend away from home or disconnected from other aspects of your life.[74] A lengthy commute or regular trips away for work can turn what seems like a reasonable commitment of hours into something far more problematic for life generally and for family life in particular. (And we'll talk more about family life in appendix 3.)

The bottom line is that once you do the audit exercise at the end of chapter 9, you will recognize (if you hadn't already) that your time is a limited resource and there are lots of relationships you have that, in light of God's metanarrative, ought to get a good slice of it.

As you process your audit results, don't shy away from asking the hard questions about your allocation of time to your paid employment. If ...

- you see the potential to add lots more people to your list and help them to Point B
- God has gifted you with the Christian convictions, character and competence to do that
- sticking with your paid employment is the only thing getting in the way

---

74 You should include how many weeks you miss church or your home group.

... why would you not search for ways to drop back to part-time employment or head into full-time paid gospel ministry?

If any aspect of your life—such as your job—is off limits to being assessed through the lens of biblical priorities, it has become an idol and needs to be smashed.

However, calling on people to smash their work or career idols seems to have become harder in recent years. Let's briefly think about why.

Vocation and the creation mandate

In Christian circles, there are two common views that I think are unhelpful when it comes to us thinking about our work (or careers).

The first is the idea that our jobs are a 'vocation' or 'calling'.

If God calls me to be a lawyer, that puts an end to it, surely? I must pursue that with all my energy and excellence, and never give it up.

But in the Bible we are not called to a *job*, but to be *followers of Jesus Christ*, and to serve him in *all* of life. Our paid employment is just one part of living out that calling. So is being a housemate, spouse, parent, church member, Point B Influencer, soccer coach, son or daughter, and so on. **If we over-prioritize our job, at the expense of all the other aspects of our Christian life, then we are not being faithful to our true calling.**

Furthermore, I might only be a soccer coach for a short period, because that's the phase of life I'm in. I'm free to give it up or continue it, depending on whether it is interfering too much with serving God in other aspects of my life. In the same way, I am free to give up my paid job. It is not a 'calling' from God; it isn't sacrosanct. If you are treating it that way, most likely it has become an idol.

We know that in his life Jesus had two jobs, and the significant one was *not* carpentry. The Bible makes absolutely no significance of that work at all, and Jesus gave it up to do something else (just like he told his disciples to give up fishing to do something else). What Jesus himself identifies as the significant calling for him was "to do the will of him who sent me and to accomplish his work" (John 4:34).

The second common idea takes one of the truths that we discussed early in this book and builds a 'theology of work' around it. It is the truth that we are made in God's image to be workers:

> "Be fruitful and multiply and fill the earth and subdue it, and have dominion over the fish of the sea and over the birds of the heavens and over every living thing that moves on the earth." (Gen 1:28)

> The LORD God took the man and put him in the garden of Eden to work it and keep it. (Gen 2:15)

God, as part of his good (i.e. pre-Fall) creation, gave man work to do and this involves the exercise of 'dominion' or 'rule' (a very broad, all-encompassing mandate). Work therefore has dignity, and, like all aspects of life, it can be done "as for the Lord" and for his glory:

> Whatever you do, work heartily, as for the Lord and not for men, knowing that from the Lord you will

receive the inheritance as your reward. You are serving the Lord Christ. (Col 3:23-24)

The basis of this view is sometimes referred to as the 'creation mandate', and there is no doubt it has something important and true to say about our work. All work can indeed be done "as for the Lord" (unless it inherently involves sinfulness). And so it is further supposed that all work is therefore of value—more than that: *equal* value. Thus the work of a doctor or a plumber is as worthwhile for Christians as choosing to be a missionary or a pastor or an evangelist.

My questions are these: Why do we base so much of this conclusion on the *creation* mandate? Why don't we uphold a *new creation* mandate? Why do we only look *backwards* to the garden of Eden to assess the value of our toil? Why don't we also look *forwards* in God's metanarrative to get a more complete picture of what God is doing and what that means for our values and choices?

It seems to me that when people look to the creation mandate to assert that all work is of equal value, they have to ignore much of the New Testament, and the way Jesus and his apostles completely radicalize our value systems and life priorities with their kingdom teaching and example.[75]

75 For more in-depth analysis of the creation mandate and how we think about work as Christians, I recommend a series of three online articles by Paul Grimmond published in *The Briefing*:
  1. 'God's plan for work: The cultural mandate', 2 July 2013 (thebriefing.com.au/2013/07/gods-plan-for-work-the-cultural-mandate)
  2. 'Vocation? What's that?', 9 September 2013 (thebriefing.com.au/2013/09/gods-plan-for-work-vocation)
  3. 'Work, value, and the gospel', 6 January 2014 (thebriefing.com.au/2014/01/work-value-and-the-gospel).

Furthermore, when looking for the fulfilment of the creation mandate—the vision of mankind subduing and having dominion over the creation—where should we turn? To the paid employment of weak and sinful people like us? Or to the risen, conquering and ascended Christ (Eph 1:20-22; 1 Cor 15:27)? If we want to work to implement the creation mandate, the effective way of doing that is by promoting Christ as Lord.

The other point worth making about the creation mandate is that on the rare occasions when the New Testament talks about reasons for doing paid work (e.g. 1 Thess 4:9-12; Eph 4:28), it doesn't use that creation mandate argument. If that view is as foundational as it is made out to be by some people, that seems odd.

Nonetheless, I think there is a way to uphold the valid truth of the creation mandate and the dignity and value it gives to human toil, while still recognizing that God's full metanarrative and Christ's lordship add an important extra dimension to our life of paid employment.

Work as an arena of ministry

If what I have outlined in the chapters of this book is true, then life and well-directed busyness is about relationship: relationship with God, and relationship with those God has placed around us. And God has revealed his metanarrative to us to enable us to discern the purpose we have in those relationships: that is, to love those people and do what we can to help them get to Point B.

Our paid employment is one *arena* of relationship. Just as our churches, our families, our neighbourhoods and our sports teams are all also arenas of relationship. They are contexts in which God brings us into contact with other people—people he cares about and desires to see transferred to the kingdom of the Son he loves and transformed in righteousness. God has placed us there in those arenas so that—in addition to working heartily ['generously'] as *for the Lord*—we can also look for opportunities to do *the work of the Lord* (i.e. proclaim Christ and live out God's message to people).[76]

In other words, the church arena is not the sole arena for your gospel ministry. Your secular workplace is an arena for that too. You are a source of light in your work colleagues' world.

This is not the book for learning how to proclaim Christ in your workplace, but I would highly recommend

---

76 The argument about whether you should do that as an architect or as a full-time pastor in many ways misses the point. What matters is how much opportunity there is to promote Christ as Lord in the arena of your job (and in other arenas of your life). Pastors are set aside for the purpose of devoting themselves "to prayer and to the ministry of the word" (Acts 6:4). This is a "noble task" and should be aspired to, respected and honoured (1 Tim 3:1; 1 Thess 5:12; 1 Tim 5:17). It is, therefore, obviously very important that we have lots of gifted pastors. However, pastors can sometimes also be so caught up with church administration that they actually end up not spending much time each week proclaiming Christ. On the other hand, some 'secular' jobs give Christians abundant opportunities. I heard recently about a soldier on deployment in a conflict zone, living 24/7 with his fellow soldiers, with lots of downtime and with their lives regularly in danger. He was able to take plenty of opportunities for proclaiming Christ in his job. How does *your* job enhance or inhibit your ability to proclaim Christ?

Craig Josling's *40 Rockets: Encouragement and tips for turbo-charging your evangelism at work.*[77]

Now, reality check time.

Your employer is not paying you to proclaim the gospel to your workmates or teach them the Bible. They are paying you to do bookkeeping, or unblock someone's drain, or fix someone's teeth, or whatever it is that you do. We are not solely in our workplace to bring God's word to people. We do have other responsibilities—competing responsibilities.

But, as they say, it is possible to walk and chew gum. It is possible both to fulfil your obligation to your employer and to biblically love your workmates. Indeed, loving your workmates is part of honouring the Lord in your workplace, and this involves not just proclaiming Christ to them, but doing your work well. In most jobs, if you don't do your work well, it unlovingly places extra burdens on your employer and your colleagues.

However, it is possible that the type or intensity of the paid work you do, and the way you are required or expected to interact with colleagues, means the opportunities for you to influence people towards Point B are minimal in your work context.

Perhaps you know that any opportunities with your colleagues will have to happen outside of work time, and

---

77 I'd also recommend William Taylor's book *Revolutionary Work: What's the point of the 9 to 5?* It is a very helpful discussion on Christians and work. While I'm recommending books, I might also mention again *The Good Sporting Life: Loving and playing sport as a follower of Jesus,* which has some very helpful things to say about how to be a faithful Christian in the arena of your sporting team.

so will decrease the time you have available to minister to people in other arenas of your life.

Thinking wisely after your chapter 9 audit exercise, you may realize that you can be more effective in ministry in those *other* arenas, and so decide you are not going to spend your scarce time on work colleagues. Or maybe you've tried sharing the gospel with them and been rejected, and you figuratively shake the dust off your feet (Matt 10:14) and move on to other more fruitful arenas. You might keep your eye out for opportunities in the future, but for the moment you decide to basically just see your work as the arena for earning money.

I think that's a valid—albeit a comparatively rare— position to come to.

However, most of us find it easier to do the transforming ministry with people who are already Christians, rather than being part of the transferring ministry with non-Christians (evangelism). As you assess your workplace as an arena for ministry, I urge you not to rationalize away any opportunities to do the latter.

Even if you can't spend a lot of time with your work colleagues, there is no reason you can't pray for them, and I suspect your responsibility for them should at least extend to that.

Appendix 2.
Church

At the end of chapter 8 I suggested that "meeting together every week with other Christians, whether at church or in a home group or one-to-one, is vitally important".

That's my starting point.

But there's more that can be usefully said.

The first such thing is to highlight again that church is one of those arenas of relationship in which we have opportunity to help people on their journey to Point B.

Unlike most secular workplaces, gospel ministry work is the primary reason we are in the church arena in the first place—it's the core purpose of church! Unlike the work arena, we not only have permission to be active in ministry at church, we hopefully are being urged, trained and encouraged to do that by our leaders.

Here's how Tony Payne puts it in his excellent little book, *How to Walk into Church*:

> Church is not about me. It's not about the experience I have or what I get out of it. Church is a classic opportunity to love my brothers and sisters who are

there, by seeking to build them up in Christ.

Of course, in many churches today it's not really like this. There's a very small number doing the building work—that is, speaking God's word to others, and encouraging others and praying—and a large majority either just gratefully accepting it, or going along for the ride.

It's the ministry of the few.

But what we're talking about, and what we see in the New Testament, is the ministry of the pew—a ministry that we all do, each Sunday, as we all seek to build one another up in love.

Is that how you think of church—as a chance to encourage, build up, love and spur on your brothers and sisters?[78]

One of the ways to build up, love and spur on your brothers and sisters at church is just to have random conversations: to see who you end up talking to, and intentionally aim to encourage them in their faith. That's certainly better than having random conversations about the football or the weather.

But there's also nothing wrong with aiming for a ministry at church that is not quite so random and unplanned. A bit of forethought on your part doesn't undermine God's providential determination of who you end up talking to; if he wants you to talk to someone in particular, no amount of planning on your part can circumvent it. (Remember chapter 2? God is never frustrated—he always achieves

78 T Payne, *How to Walk into Church*, Matthias Media, 2015, pp 32-33.

what he wants to achieve.)

So there's nothing wrong with thinking through in advance (and praying about) the people you particularly hope to encourage:

- "I know Jason has been struggling with poor health recently, so I will make a point of asking him how he is going and praying with him."
- "I think Jess is starting her new job tomorrow, so I will let her know I will be praying for her and encourage her to find a way in her first week to let some of her new work colleagues know she is a Christian."
- "Warren has missed the last two weeks of home group, so I will check in, make sure he's okay, and see if he wants to read through together the passages he missed before our next home group meeting."

Do you walk into church with a list like that in your head, if not on paper? If church is an arena for consciously helping people move towards Point B, going to church is not a passive exercise.

I would particularly encourage you to think about people in church as you do your audit exercise at the end of chapter 9. Who are the one, two or three people at church that you should consider including on your list? Perhaps because you have a good rapport with them. Perhaps because you can see they need a bit of spiritual help. Perhaps because they have potential to help others and you want to get them started along that path. Perhaps because they are the teenagers you lead in youth group. Put them on your list and think through how much time you can invest in them and what might be helpful to their growth.

Think also about whether you can achieve what you want to achieve with those people just in the time before and after church, or whether you might need to set up some other time during the week (e.g. to read the Bible one-to-one with them).[79]

Over-busy with church

Since church is so important, we rightly ought to be busy in the church arena. Sunday church, midweek home group, music ministry, committee of management, leading prayers, and of course personal ministry to others— these are all important sorts of things to commit yourself joyfully to.

A word of caution though. The needs of your church are almost limitless, and filling them is often sufficiently enjoyable (at least some of the time) for us to end up spending a high proportion of our discretionary time on church activities. Some of us also immediately feel guilty if any need is mentioned in our church, and we seem to have a very limited capacity to say 'no' to our church leaders.

As we will discuss shortly, the church ministry you take on can often be at the expense of your ministry to your own family, or, perhaps more commonly, your ministry to non-Christians in your various life arenas. In fact, for many of us, we end up spending very little of our discretionary time with non-Christians at all; we even play sport

---

79 See David Helm's useful book *One-to-One Bible Reading: A simple guide for every Christian*.

with our Christian friends.

Those non-Christian people in your life are on a path to destruction, and whilst that doesn't necessarily always trump all other forms of ministry, it ought to make us pause and think hard about the need to carve out *some* of our time for spending with them in the hope of saving them from God's punishment.

I particularly despair when Christians who seem to have a gift for evangelism end up being loaded with church ministries, and thus end up with very limited capacity for exercising their important evangelistic gift. If you're a pastor, I urge you to refrain from doing that to your evangelistically gifted people.[80] If you're one of those gifted people, talk to your pastor about supporting you in your evangelism.

But with that caveat on the table, I don't want to end this section without urging you to busy yourself with gospel ministry in your church. It's an arena of choice for all Christians.

---

80 For more on this, see Roger Carswell's book *And Some Evangelists: Growing your church through discovering and developing evangelists*, especially chapter 10.

Appendix 3.
Family life

Just like work and church, family life is another arena of relationship in which we have opportunity to work to help people on their journey towards Point B, the new creation, the eternal kingdom of God.

As we discussed with work, family life can look quite different for each of us.

For example, you may be a mature single person without any kids. You still have family, perhaps parents, siblings, and others. But you don't live with your family any more.

Or, like me, you might have adult children who no longer live with you. My 'household' consists of my wife and myself. Yet I still think of my two adult children as my family. I also think of my son-in-law and grandson as 'family'.[81]

Or you may be a teenager or young adult, still living with your parents and siblings.

---

81 This was my family at the time of writing. That's the thing about family—it may change from time to time.

The possibilities are many and varied. But there is a truth that I think is still universal, which is that we have a higher responsibility towards our family:

> Honour widows who are truly widows. But if a widow has children or grandchildren, let them first learn to show godliness to their own household and to make some return to their parents, for this is pleasing in the sight of God. She who is truly a widow, left all alone, has set her hope on God and continues in supplications and prayers night and day, but she who is self-indulgent is dead even while she lives. Command these things as well, so that they may be without reproach. But if anyone does not provide for his relatives, and especially for members of his household, he has denied the faith and is worse than an unbeliever. (1 Tim 5:3-8)

Although in the context Paul here seems to be talking mainly about providing for the daily *physical* necessities of family members, some of these words show he is also concerned for the *spiritual* welfare of widows (widows being a specific type of family member who may need help).

Certainly with regard to our parents, the obligation to care and provide for them flows from a wider biblical obligation to honour them (one of the Ten Commandments of course: Exod 20:12; cf. Eph 6:2-3).

Parents are likewise responsible to care for their children, a responsibility that is assumed to be obvious, even for us who are "evil":

"Or which one of you, if his son asks him for bread, will give him a stone? Or if he asks for a fish, will give him a serpent? If you then, who are evil, know how to give good gifts to your children, how much more will your Father who is in heaven give good things to those who ask him!" (Matt 7:9-11)

But the spiritual development of children is specifically mentioned in Ephesians:

Fathers, do not provoke your children to anger, but bring them up in the discipline and instruction of the Lord. (Eph 6:4)

In other words, fathers (in particular) have the job of helping their kids along their journey to Point B. However, there is little doubt that this responsibility is also part of a mother's task of loving her children (Titus 2:4), which older women are to help her learn to do.

However, the responsibility and relationship is not reciprocal between parents and children (even financially; cf. 2 Cor 12:14). While parents may teach and lead their children towards maturity in the faith, the dynamics of children leading their parents is more problematic. Indeed, younger people teaching and leading older people takes more sensitivity and has to come with due respect. That's why Paul encourages Timothy not to "rebuke an older man, but encourage him" (1 Tim 5:1). Relating to older women and younger women also needs to be done in an appropriate way that recognizes the age difference (1 Tim 5:2).

For those of you with unbelieving parents, you are

probably already aware of how difficult it is to help them come to know the Lord Jesus. Like me, you've probably already made relational mistakes in your enthusiasm to see that happen.

It takes a very high degree of humility, and of course a powerful work of the Spirit, for a parent to have their worldview changed by listening attentively to what their child has learned.

In terms of siblings, I can't find too much in the Bible about our responsibility to care for them, other than the general care responsibilities of family mentioned already (i.e. 1 Tim 5:8). But it would be a strange thing indeed if we cared for, encouraged and grew others as our brothers and sisters in Christ, but didn't do that for our *actual* brothers and sisters.

Then, of course, for many of us there is the husband and wife relationship. This is one the Bible obviously says a lot about, including Ephesians 5, where the husband is given responsibility to love his wife "in the same way" as Christ loved the church—that is, with an intent to present her to Christ "in splendour, without spot or wrinkle or any such thing, that she might be holy and without blemish" (vv 25-28). The goal is to help her get to Point B, and to get her there with a wonderful degree of conformity to the likeness of Christ.

The bottom line is this: while some family responsibilities are closer and higher than others,[82] family members

---

82 E.g. a husband's responsibility for his wife or a parent's responsibility for a child might be greater than a child's responsibility for a sibling.

ought to be among the top priorities on the list that flows out of our chapter 9 audit exercise.

Let me say a little in turn about busyness and the relationship with a spouse, children, siblings, and parents—particularly as it relates to the goal of helping them get to Point B.

Spouse

This is not a book on marriage, nor am I particularly qualified to give marriage advice—unless you want advice about how to be married to my wife, in which case I have decades of experience.[83]

But this *is* a book on busyness, so let me make a few brief observations about marriage and that topic.

Once again, it is worth stating the obvious: we are all different, and our marriages reflect our different personalities. One married couple might consider themselves total soulmates and do everything together. Other couples would find that a disastrous way to relate, and frequently need some space.

Having said that, we are not free to say, "Oh, that's just not who I am!" As we have already seen, part of being in family life is accepting responsibilities for meeting the needs of others, and it is impossible to do that well without allowing time for it.

For a husband, that means taking the lead in making sure you as a couple are both growing in Christian maturity on your journey to Point B.

83 Actually, I'm hoping you don't want that advice.

Reading the Bible and praying together is a key part (but by no means the totality) of fulfilling that responsibility. But I know from personal experience that doing those basics is a challenge in busy lives, with different and demanding respective schedules, and with different personalities and learning styles.

If there's not much happening between you and your spouse in this area, here are some quick tips:

- Make a start, aim low and build from there. So don't aim for an hour-long daily Bible and prayer session. Start by committing to 5 minutes of prayer together before you head off to work each day. Maybe then add 5 minutes of reading a Bible devotional resource before you pray. Perhaps add one evening/morning a week when you spend a bit more time, say half an hour, reading the Bible and praying.[84] Then maybe step up to two evenings/mornings a week, and so on. Bear in mind that they say it takes a while for a new routine to become a habit, so really work hard to stick to each stage for a good while.[85]

---

84 If you're in a home group, you could either read the Bible passage before the study or review it together after the study.

85 Google this and you'll find lots of different answers as to how many days it takes to form a habit. The top search result I got suggested a range from 18 to 254 days, which doesn't seem like a very helpful answer. Others suggest 66 days is the average. I suspect the 21/90 day rule is helpful and seems about right: do it for 21 days straight, by which time it is starting to form into a habit. At that point, renew your commitment for a further 90 days to really cement it in as part of your way of life.

- Wives, can I please suggest you don't hold back from initiating prayer and Bible reading out of some misguided interpretation of 'submission' to your husband's leadership? I have heard some women suggest that since it is the man's responsibility to lead, for her to initiate the activity is usurping the man's role. Hmm, I'm not convinced. Blokes are sinful, distracted, forgetful and, as a massive generalization, not as wired for relational activity as women. If you can help your husband by encouraging prayer and Bible reading, I say do it! Maybe don't do it in an accusing way: "Hey, John reads the Bible with Anna every day. Why can't you be more like him?!"[86] Maybe something more like: "Hey, I'd love to pray with you about X, Y and Z before we head off this morning. Have you got time?"

- Recognize that reading the Bible together often involves a compromise. Your preferred methods might be quite different. At the moment, my wife and I have been finding the Swedish Method a really good way to read the Bible together.[87]

86 Or "Hey, you haven't initiated prayer for 17 days in a row. What gives, you pagan Son of Adam?!"

87 For more information see Peter Blowes's *Briefing* article 'The Swedish Method', 1 January 2009 (thebriefing.com.au/2009/01/the-swedish-method).

- If you have kids, it's helpful for them to see you and your spouse reading the Bible and praying together.[88] If they demand your attention, try appealing to their better nature: "Mummy and Daddy are trying to spend some time with God. Can you play quietly on your own just for a very little while and then we can do something together?" As a couple, make one of your discussion points from the Bible answering the question: "How could we share this truth with our kids?"

- As the late John Chapman used to suggest, invest in that marvellous devotional aid: the alarm clock.[89] In other words, don't make a habit of sleeping in when you ought to be getting up and spending time with God.

Of course, there are more options available for building each other up in maturity than these basic staples of prayer and Bible reading: working and praying together as a ministry team in other 'arenas', especially church; going to a Christian conference or camp together; regu-

---

88 As one mother put it: "I know in our family, we find going to church easy to prioritize, but we have at times neglected our personal Bible reading and studying God's word together as a family. In our kids' little years, and even now as two of them are at school, our personal Bible reading has almost always been out of sight of our children. Since lockdown last year, I've become more and more convinced that my children witnessing me regularly reading God's word and praying is one of the most powerful ways to disciple them and encourage them in their own spiritual disciplines as they grow up." Gemma Bartlett, 'Learning from home: An opportunity to teach what matters', *Growing Faith*, 30 July 2021, accessed 22 February 2022 (growingfaith.com.au/articles/learning-from-home-an-opportunity-to-teach-what-matters).

89 For the benefit of younger readers, an alarm clock is an old technology that pre-dates the mobile phone. It was dual function: it told you the time *and* it rang a bell at (roughly) the time you set it for. ⏰

larly talking through your chapter 9 audit results; reading Christian books; being in a home group together or at least talking together about what you are each learning in your respective groups; spending time together with non-Christian friends and working together in conversation to create gospel opportunities ... all of these keep us focused on serving and growing in the Lord Jesus.

But they all take time. And they can all too easily be crowded out by the tyranny of the urgent or just the relentlessness of the day-to-day stuff of modern life. In the developed world we have so many options available to us that use up our time. That's why intentionality is so vital. We will only say 'yes' to the activities that reflect "well-directed busyness" if we say 'no' to the thousands of other—often good—activities that get in the way.

Intentionality is also a key to maintaining a healthy physical side to your relationship. Married couples are instructed in the Bible to have sex regularly (1 Cor 7:1-5). Now, being told to have sex doesn't sound very spontaneous and romantic. But perhaps God actually knows something about how these things work. If you wait for spontaneity, you will end up waiting a long time; the reality is that the longer you have been married, the less likely something unpredictable is going to happen. In fact, in some (quite long) phases of married life, the thing that is more likely to be spontaneous is a child interrupting you.

So, as you plan out how you will care for and carve out time for your spouse, make sure you plan time and opportunities for intimacy. (Surely the whole new 'working from home' regime has to have some hidden perks!)

Children

Babies and children are a busyness machine—precision-engineered to achieve optimum calorie input to busyness output ratios. They look so innocent and adorable, but they produce busyness by the truck load. From Day 1, your regular plan and schedule is out the window and being deconstructed and reconstructed by this new family member. From my experience, this state of affairs pretty much lasts until they learn to drive.

Adding a second child doesn't necessarily double the busyness, depending on whether you can find some economies of scale. From what I am told—and this is certainly not something my wife and I ever wished to research for ourselves—the parent busyness level doesn't start stabilizing until the fifth, sixth or seventh child, by which time the oldest children can actually be useful in helping with the youngest.

To use a well-worn metaphor, we all juggle quite a few balls in life. Naturally, having children significantly adds to the number of balls. But these balls are also oddly shaped and weighted, so when juggling them they tend to act in unpredictable ways in the air—ways that make the whole juggling exercise far more challenging.

So as parents there is a period of 20-plus years in which your busyness/juggling will be intense and potentially stressful. And there are two things that will exacerbate that stress experience:

1. being over-ambitious about what you will achieve
2. being over-ambitious about what your children will achieve.

1. Over-ambition for ourselves as parents

As the apostle Paul points out, the single person is different to the married person (who I think is probably presumed to have a family, not just a spouse). The married person's "interests are divided" (1 Cor 7:34); they can't have the same focus on and capacity for serving the Lord in non-family 'arenas' that a single person can have. Failure to recognize this truth can lead a new parent to be over-ambitious about the amount of ministry or work they can continue to do.

Yes, you can push hard to try to achieve a lot in your work or ministry in this parenting season of life, and try moulding your family life around it. And it *might* work. But you and your baby are most likely *not* the exception to the rule; the statistics are against you, so do be realistic in your ambitions, even godly ones.

Having said that, being a parent is not an excuse to drop out of doing ministry. There's a balance: some of us need to push harder and not be so inwardly focused on our family, whereas some of us have to be reminded of our theology of God's sovereignty (i.e. he can get things done at church without you if he needs to).

2. Over-ambition for our children

Over the past few decades, however, parents have also become much more ambitious about *what their children might achieve.*

We talked in chapter 5 about 'YOLO'. A related term is 'FOMO'—the Fear Of Missing Out (i.e. on positive life experiences). I think I want to coin a new acronym:

FOMKMO—Fear Of My Kids Missing Out. This fear very naturally plays on the heartstrings of any loving parent.

It is also a fear that manifests in the multiplication of activities in which our children are participating. Indeed, schools market themselves these days based on the 'enriched learning experience' they offer our kids. On top of that, we rush around taking them to extra-curricular activities after school: one, two or even three team sports, music lessons, dance classes, tutoring, karate, concert experiences, computer coding and more.

Child psychologists call it 'over-scheduling', and they don't like it. It frequently produces stressed parents, stressed kids, anxiety and even depression in both. The idea that 'the earlier they start, the better' in acquiring some skill that promises them success as an adult is frequently misguided and often unhelpful to a child's wellbeing.

In his book *The Hurried Child: Growing up too fast too soon*, David Elkind identifies and laments all the different ways we hurry and accelerate our children. What he highlights is worrying and challenging. But to my mind the harshest reality he points out is the way it can be perceived by our children:

> Young children (two to eight years) tend to perceive hurrying as a rejection, as evidence that their parents do not really care about them. Children are very emotionally astute in this regard and tune in to what is a partial truth. To a certain extent, hurrying children from one caretaker to another each day, or into academic achievement, or into making decisions they are not really able to make *is* a rejection.

It is a rejection of the children as they see themselves, of what they are capable of coping with and doing. Children find such rejection very threatening and often develop stress symptoms as a result.[90]

Steve Biddulph, the psychologist/author whom I referred to earlier when talking about 'work', has this useful and memorable slogan at the top of his website: "Hurry is the enemy of love".[91]

Elkind actually suggests that the solution to childhood stress is time to play:

> Basically, play is nature's way of dealing with stress for children as well as adults. As parents, we can help by investing in toys and playthings that give the greatest scope to the child's imagination.[92]

Our society, and schools in particular, tend to encourage this 'hurrying' of our children, all of which adds to our family busyness. We can agitate against it, but we will be fighting a massive cultural force, and we're not likely to win and change the society around us.

However, as parents we have a choice within our family arena. We control that arena (at least we do if we can resist the peer pressure of other parents). We can choose not to suffer from FOMKMO. Neither we, nor our kids, need to live our best life now. We have a new and even better life to look forward to (Point B). Not many of those

90 D Elkind, *The Hurried Child: Growing up too fast too soon*, 3rd edn, Perseus Publishing, 2001, pp 207-208.
91 See stevebiddulph.com, accessed 9 February 2022.
92 Elkind, *The Hurried Child*, p 218.

FOMKMO experiences are going to have much positive bearing on that future. Indeed, they more often have a greater potential to derail our kids from that future.

Instead, let the kids play; it's good for them and it'll ease your parental busyness. Just as importantly, it will open up more space for fulfilling the parental responsibility to "bring them up in the discipline and instruction of the Lord" (Eph 6:4). That task can be done in a structured way and an unstructured one.

In terms of structures, you will want to extend the Bible reading and prayer habit you have developed with your spouse to include your child/children. Again, this is not the book to explore the ins and outs of how to do that well. I warmly recommend *Bible Reading with Your Kids: A simple guide for every father* by Jon Nielson. In terms of teaching very young children (1 to 4-year-olds), and involving them in prayer, I'm going to engage in a little nepotism and recommend my own wife Stephanie's series, Books for Little Ones, and the accompanying online notes for parents.[93] Commit to a regular time of doing this structured teaching and modelling.

However, there is an unstructured way of training and instructing our children that takes advantage of the little opportunities each day when we can bring God into our child's consciousness. It involves keeping an eye out for those 'teaching moments' that actually turn out to be very frequent when you are actively looking for them. You see this idea in the book of Deuteronomy:

93 For a list of books in the series, see matthiasmedia.com/bflo.

And these words that I command you today shall be on your heart. You shall teach them diligently to your children, and shall talk of them when you sit in your house, and when you walk by the way, and when you lie down, and when you rise. (Deut 6:6-7)

Young children don't necessarily thrive on heavy-content Bible lessons and lengthy prayer times. Far more impactful will be the frequent, brief, but natural inclusion of the things of God in our conversations with them throughout the day—when you sit in your house, when you're driving in the car, over the breakfast table. The ability to spot those opportunities and use them really only develops with practice, and once you've mastered the art, it remains very useful into a child's teenage years.

Siblings

If you've read this far, you can probably guess what my opening remark is going to be already, but I'll say it anyway: the sorts of relationships people have with their siblings are many and varied.

You may be an only child (you get an early mark, and can skip to the next section!). Like me, you may have just one sibling. Or you may have ... well, Guinness World Records asserts that an 18th-century Russian peasant had 69 children.[94] So I think I'm safe in assuming you have

94 Sixteen pairs of twins, seven sets of triplets and four sets of quadruplets —and that was just his first wife. His second wife was comparatively unproductive: a mere 18 children. See Guinness World Records, *Most prolific mother ever*, Guinness World Records website, 2022, accessed 9 February 2022 (guinnessworldrecords.com/world-records/most-prolific-mother-ever).

fewer than 68 siblings. In Australia, the current average is one sibling (i.e. two children in the family).

But it is more than just the number of siblings that varies. Some siblings have an ultra-close bond even into adulthood, and hardly a day goes by when they don't talk to each other and share what is happening in their lives. Other siblings live very separate lives, sometimes because of geography, sometimes because they don't have that much in common, sometimes because there has been relational breakdown at some point.

When I start typing 'sibling' into a search engine, it lists 'sibling rivalry' above 'sibling love' as the auto-complete suggestion. I think that possibly tells you everything you need to know about the troublesome relationships we often have with our siblings.

Of course, you don't have to read very far in the Bible to see evidence of that, although I hope the murder of Abel by Cain (Genesis 4) is an unusually hostile example.[95]

I suspect it's actually going to be fairly unusual for a sibling relationship to be a significant contributor to our busyness. So most of the thoughts that follow are more about how we can help our siblings on their journey to Point B, rather than how to manage the time such relationships take up.

---

95 But bear in mind Jesus' teaching about the close heart connection of anger and murder: "You have heard that it was said to those of old, 'You shall not murder; and whoever murders will be liable to judgement.' But I say to you that everyone who is angry with his brother will be liable to judgement; whoever insults his brother will be liable to the council; and whoever says, 'You fool!' will be liable to the hell of fire" (Matt 5:21-22).

It's probably worth distinguishing between some common scenarios: (i) where you have grown up in a Christian home and your siblings are fellow believers (albeit in different stages of maturity), and (ii) where you have not grown up in a Christian home and your siblings are not believers. I will also talk briefly about the difficult scenario (iii) when you have grown up in a Christian home but one of your siblings has wandered from the faith (as a teen or adult).

Writing as someone who didn't grow up in a Christian home, can I remind those of you who did what an enormous privilege you had/have? What a privilege that your brothers/sisters and parents can be your brothers/sisters in Christ. I know they are sinful and can be as frustrating as unbelievers at times, but don't let that get in the way of appreciating the bond of fellowship you have in Christ. You have that bond whether you take the time to enjoy it or not. So take the time to enjoy it, I reckon.

If you want to grow your relationship with your sibling, can I suggest you pray for and with them? And tell them you pray for them. (And I don't mean do this when they have annoyed you: "Ugh, I pray for you, you despicable wretch!") Maybe even read the Bible with them—not in place of parents doing that, but as a bonus. (This will tend to be more likely from teenagehood, when kids start to read the Bible for themselves instead of with their mums and dads.)

That sort of ministry within your family arena can be a very powerful one, especially if you are the older sibling. As much as we younger siblings hate to admit it, we often look up to our older siblings, especially if the age gap is a couple of years or more. An older sibling can have a profound spiritual influence on a younger sibling, one which your Christian parents will be *very* thankful for. Of course, that's not to say that in God's providential plan he hasn't been known to reverse things so that the younger sibling ends up leading the older (see Rom 9:12).

Jumping briefly to scenario (iii), in which one of your siblings has wandered from the faith, your Christian parents will be even more thankful for your efforts to guide your sibling back to the faith. Being a parent in that situation is tough; *very* tough. Parents are in an authority relationship with their children, but the child who wanders from the faith is, in one sense, rebelling and rejecting that authority. It is a difficult dynamic in which to try to win a child back to the faith. Generally all that parents can do is love their wayward child and pray for them. Perhaps they can encourage them at points. But challenging, let alone rebuking, their child is rarely a helpful strategy.

You, however, as a sibling, can push a bit harder. You do not have the same complex authority relationship with your wayward sibling.

While that sibling is rebelling, you are quite possibly going to be the person most likely to be able to influence them back. Stick close; talk to them about what's going on in their lives and what they are thinking or feeling; ask, ask, ask and listen, listen, listen. But you can also offer to help with their doubts and questions; you can push and challenge, and even tell them forthrightly when they are being foolish (that's what siblings do, right?!).

The same is true in our scenario (ii), where you have not grown up in a Christian home, and you long for your siblings (and parents—but we'll talk about them in a moment) to come to know Christ and his salvation. Although your non-Christian parents are unlikely to be quite so thankful for it, it is still true that you are the person most likely to be able to share the gospel with your siblings. Your unbelieving siblings ought to be high on your list of people to give time to after your chapter 9 audit exercise.

The unfortunate reality, however, is that they are the ones who are also most likely to know all the ungodly things you do which don't quite square with your professed faith. And they *will* bring them up and use them against you! So swallow your pride, be humble, admit your failings, repent, ask for forgiveness when those things have hurt your sibling, and press on to show that Jesus came to heal the sick, not the healthy:

> And when Jesus heard it, he said to them, "Those who are well have no need of a physician, but those who are sick. I came not to call the righteous, but sinners." (Mark 2:17)

Anecdotally, I think one child becoming a Christian has a smallish impact on unbelieving parents. When a second or third child in the family follows their sibling's lead and also becomes a Christian, parents—humanly speaking at least—are more likely to be influenced in that direction as well.

Parents

So ... let's talk about parents.

How much our parents contribute to our busyness as adults will vary, often with significant cultural factors coming into play, as well as health issues (particularly as our parents get older).

As I mentioned before, there are very clear, God-given responsibilities we have that don't really leave us a lot of room for saying to them, "Sorry; I have other priorities". Having said that, reading Matthew 10:37 and 12:46-50 and Luke 9:61-62 will alert you to the great need for wisdom in balancing these family responsibilities with a commitment to wider kingdom mission.

Given the individual circumstances and different expectations, it's hard to talk too much about how much time to give to our relationships with our parents, so let's focus instead on how we can be 'influencers' in their lives.

Generally, and rightly, parents are the leaders in your family arena: always older than you (not counting a rare step-parent scenario), and rightly expecting your respect and deference. That's the normal dynamic at play in a parent/child relationship. And, as we've discussed earlier, it's very much a biblical dynamic.

Let's start by talking about believing parents.

There is honour due to your Christian parents. And as we've seen, the way we relate to them needs to be respectful, leaning more towards encouragement than rebuke (1 Tim 5:1).

However, it is also reasonable to expect that Christian parents understand that there is a higher authority: God and his word. And they know that even infants can speak the truth (Matt 21:14-16). Is it therefore possible for a child to teach his or her parents? Yes, I think so, by using God's word—in a humble rather than arrogant way.

We probably ought to see that as an unusual scenario —a child teaching a parent. But it might be, for example, as your parents are facing a serious health situation or unemployment, that you can helpfully draw their attention to a reassuring Bible truth.

But on the whole, I think teaching and wisdom is generally passed in the direction of parent to child, not the other way around. So appreciatively welcoming that input from your Christian parents, rather than rolling your eyes when they offer it, is the attitude to foster. And pray for them to keep growing and maturing in Christlikeness, and serving faithfully as they get older; catching up with them regularly to see how they are going and to encourage them along. (By the way, one of the best ways to encourage them is to report in on what God is doing in your own life.)

But what about *unbelieving* parents and that complex relational dynamic?

How are *you* going to teach them a whole new worldview (Christian), different to the one they have lived with for 40, 50, 60+ years, given the normal parental dynamic? Answer: you're almost certainly *not* going to.

As I said before, it takes a very high degree of humility, and of course a powerful work of the Spirit, for a parent to have their worldview revolutionized by listening to what their child has learned.[96]

It's true, of course, that your repentant life itself can be a powerful witness. But when we rely solely on our life to be our witness, it by and large fails, because the gospel is a message that needs to be conveyed in words, not just actions. Actions require interpretation, and most non-Christians don't have the biblical framework to interpret your godly actions around the home and come up with "My child is responding with faithful acts of thankful obedience to the atoning work of Christ on the cross for his/her forgiveness and Christ's resurrection to be the eternal ruler and judge of the world". Don't get me wrong; you should still work hard to be godly and loving, as it will be way more persuasive than your ungodliness when gospel words do end up being communicated to your parents. Nothing turns unbelievers off more than the hypocrisy of the Christians they know, and close family members tend to see our hypocrisy more than anyone.

In the end, you as a son or daughter telling your unbelieving parents what they should believe is really not likely to be very fruitful. However, offering them an opportunity to learn what it is that drew you to the Christian faith *might* be better received:

> Hey, Mum, the last thing I ever want to do is come across as the family Bible-basher. But if you ever

96 But I've also noticed something happens with the next generation. Grandchildren often have a special place in their grandparents' hearts, and so receive much greater leniency. That can sometimes result in a more positive response to a grandchild's gentle efforts to share the gospel with them.

want to understand what drew me to the Christian faith, I'd be happy for you to come with me to church, or to give you a book that explains my new faith, or sit down with you and read some of the Bible that has really influenced my thinking.

It's that sort of tone that I think has the most chance of being accepted—as opposed to saying something that implies they've got it all wrong and you're going to set them right (e.g. "If you bothered to read the Bible for yourself, you'd see that Jesus isn't who you think he is").

But here's the bottom line: nothing is going to open your parents' hearts to the truth of Jesus without the work of the Holy Spirit removing their blindness. So your primary job is to pray for your parents. And, motivated by the future judgement they face, to do it "without ceasing" (1 Thess 5:17). Let me tell you a true story to encourage you to do that.

My friend Grant became a Christian as a young man. His parents were not Christians, and even though Grant was a fine evangelist, he found it near impossible to talk to his mum and dad about his faith. Nonetheless, he resolved from a young age to pray for them every day.

Decades later, Grant's elderly mother developed a terminal illness. So Grant prayed for courage, and said, "Mum, you know I'm a Christian. I was wondering if you would be willing to talk together about God and for me to share some of the Bible with you when I take you to your specialist appointments?"

To his great surprise and delight she said yes. As his mother's condition worsened and she was hospitalized,

Grant sat by her bed reading the Bible, explaining the gospel and praying with her. After returning home one time, Grant received a call from the hospital to say his mother had had a bad turn and he needed to come. Grant knew this was probably his last chance, so he pleaded with God to keep his mum alive until he arrived, when he would tell her the good news again. The Lord graciously did that, and he shared the gospel one last time. God blessed his efforts in a beautiful way, with his mum coming to faith by praying a prayer expressing her trust in the Lord Jesus. She died very soon after.

Grant's father then came to live with Grant and his family. Grant figured he ought to talk to his dad about the gospel too. So one day, he went into the family room, sat down next to his dad and said, "Hey Dad, you know how I visited Mum, and we talked about God, and she eventually put her trust in Jesus before she died? Well, I was thinking it might be good for you and me to talk about it too. What do you think?"

"Oh," said Grant's dad, "yes, I was there in the room listening in to your conversation all those times. And I prayed the same prayer as your mum."

As is so often the case for long-married widowers, it was not long after that Grant's father also passed away.

In God's kindness, Grant's daily prayers over decades were answered, and at a point when he really had little human hope that his parents would be saved.

So don't give up praying for your parents, and keep an eye out for an opportunity that God opens up for you to share the gospel with them.

But, being conscious of the challenges involved in evangelizing your own parents, you might also regularly pray that God will bring other faithful and loving Christians across their paths too.

Even amidst the brokenness that all too frequently accompanies our relationship with our parents, they normally hold a special place in our hearts. They ought rightly be towards the top of our chapter 9 audit list, and receive a good allocation of our time, particularly if they are not (yet!) Christians.

Feedback on this resource

We really appreciate getting feedback about our resources—not just suggestions for how to improve them, but also positive feedback and ways they can be used. We especially love to hear that the resources may have helped someone in their Christian growth.

You can send feedback to us via the 'Feedback' menu in our online store, or write to us at info@matthiasmedia.com.au.

✿ matthiasmedia

thias Media is an evangelical publishing ministry that seeks to persuade Christians of the truth of God's purposes in Jesus Christ as revealed in Bible, and equip them with high-quality resources, so that by the work he Holy Spirit they will:

- abandon their lives to the honour and service of Christ in daily holiness and decision-making
- pray constantly in Christ's name for the fruitfulness and growth of his gospel
- speak the Bible's life-changing word whenever and however they can— in the home, in the world and in the fellowship of his people.

r resources range includes Bible studies, books, training courses, tracts d children's material. To find out more, and to access samples and free wnloads, visit our website:

www.matthiasmedia.com

ow to buy our resources

Direct from us over the internet:
– in the US: www.matthiasmedia.com
– in Australia: www.matthiasmedia.com.au

Direct from us by phone: please visit our website
for current phone contact information.

Through a range of outlets in various parts of the world.
Visit **www.matthiasmedia.com/contact**
for details about recommended retailers in your part of the world.

Trade enquiries can be addressed to:
– in the US and Canada: sales@matthiasmedia.com
– in Australia and the rest of the world: sales@matthiasmedia.com.au

Register at our website for our **free** regular email update to receive information about the latest new resources, **exclusive special offers**, and free
articles to help you grow in your Christian life and ministry.

Also from Matthias Media

When the Noise Won't Stop

A Christian guide to dealing with anxiety
by Paul Grimmond

When the Noise Won't Stop combines deep personal experience and comprehensive biblical study to demonstrate how the gospel addresses the pain and difficulty of anxiety. Avoiding simplistic answers while candidly sharing his own struggles, Paul Grimmond shows readers how the good news of Jesus offers light and promise to those who are suffering. His in-depth consideration of how the Bible forms and addresses our understanding of anxiety provides much-needed encouragement for Christians dealing personally with an anxiety disorder and for Christians caring for someone with this growing societal problem.

For more information or to order contact:

Matthias Media
Email: sales@matthiasmedia.com.au
www.matthiasmedia.com.au

Matthias Media (USA)
Email: sales@matthiasmedia.com
www.matthiasmedia.com

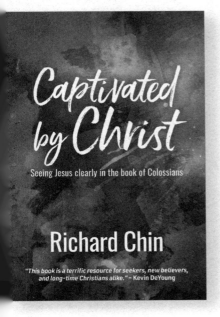